These Flowers Belong to:

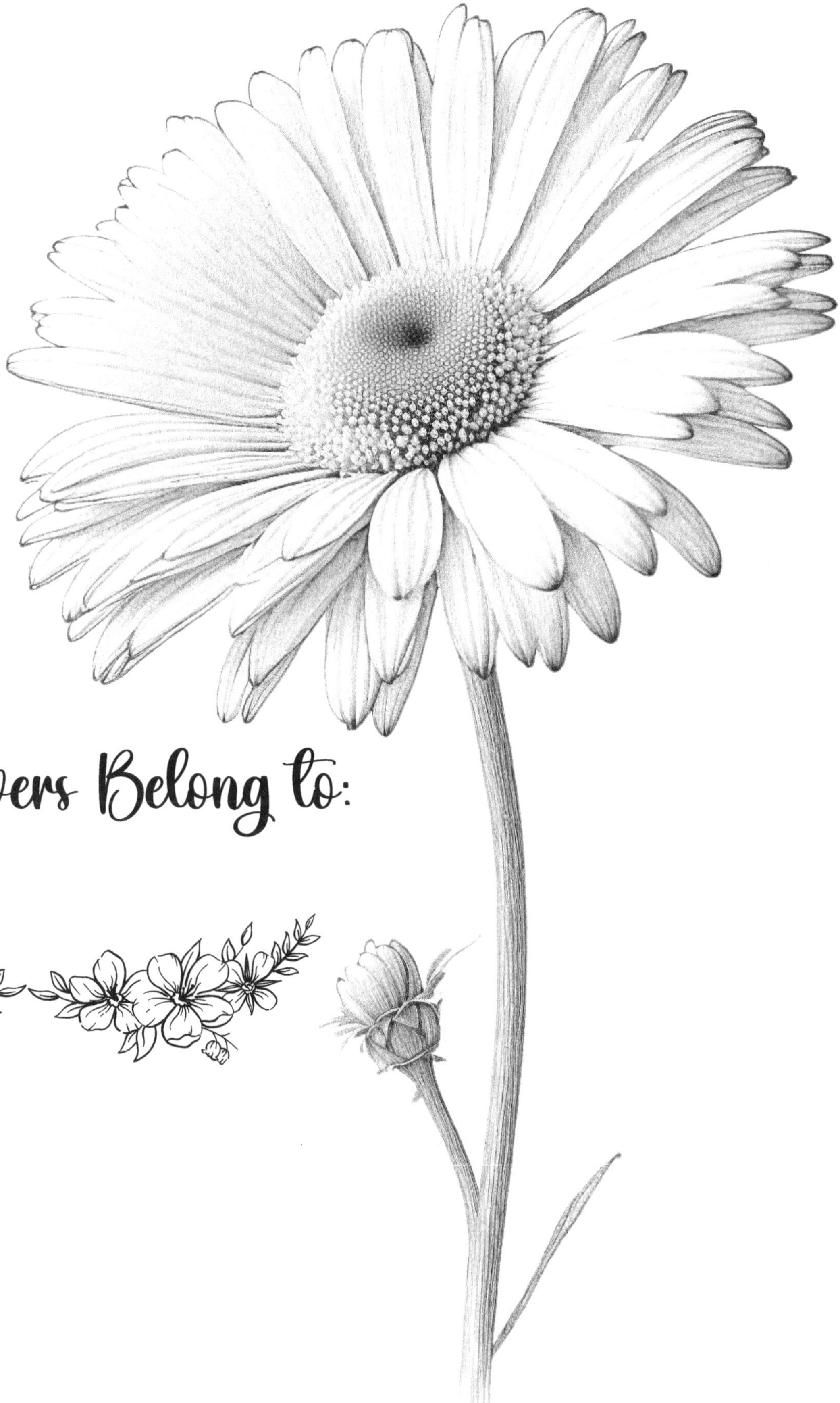

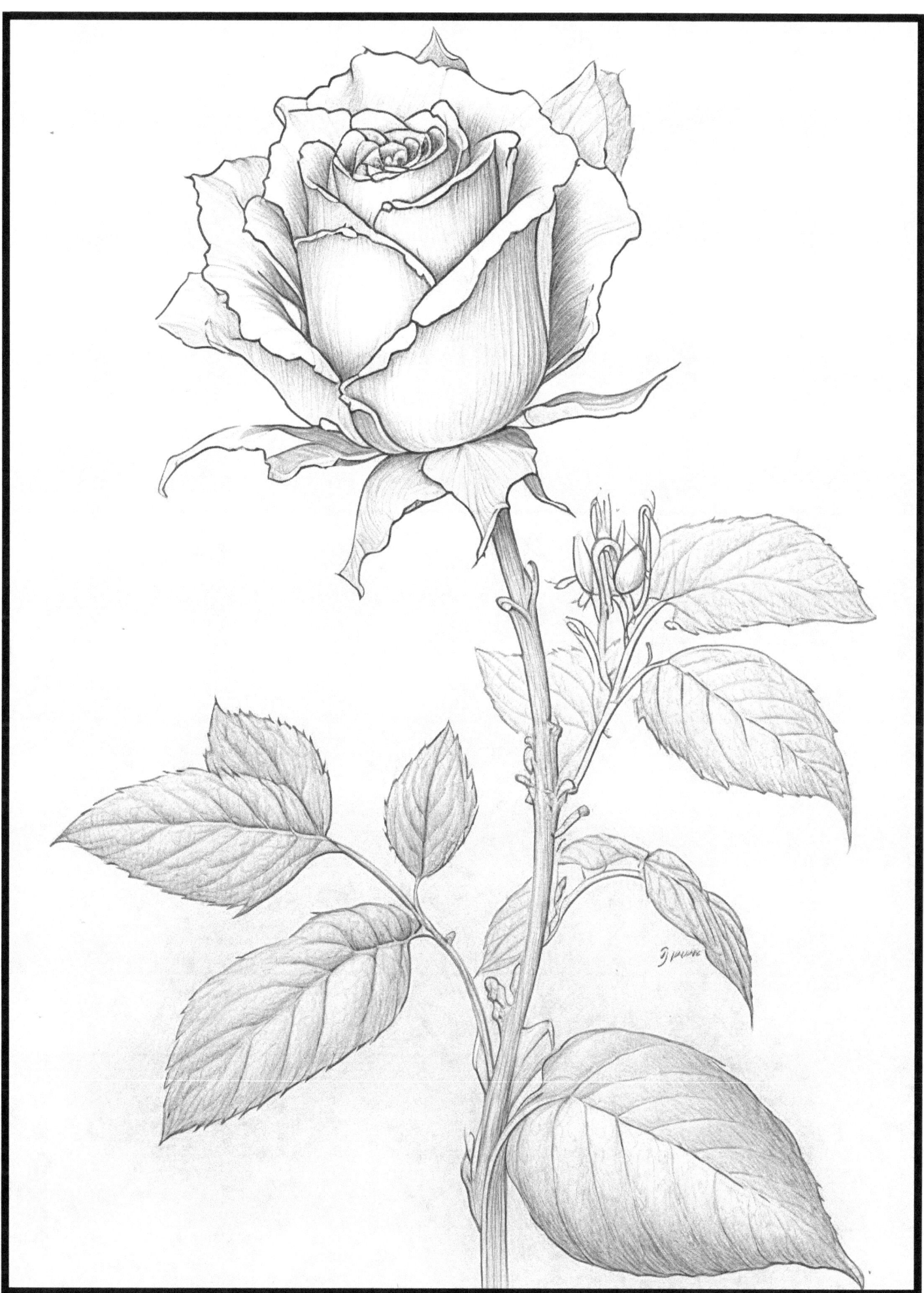

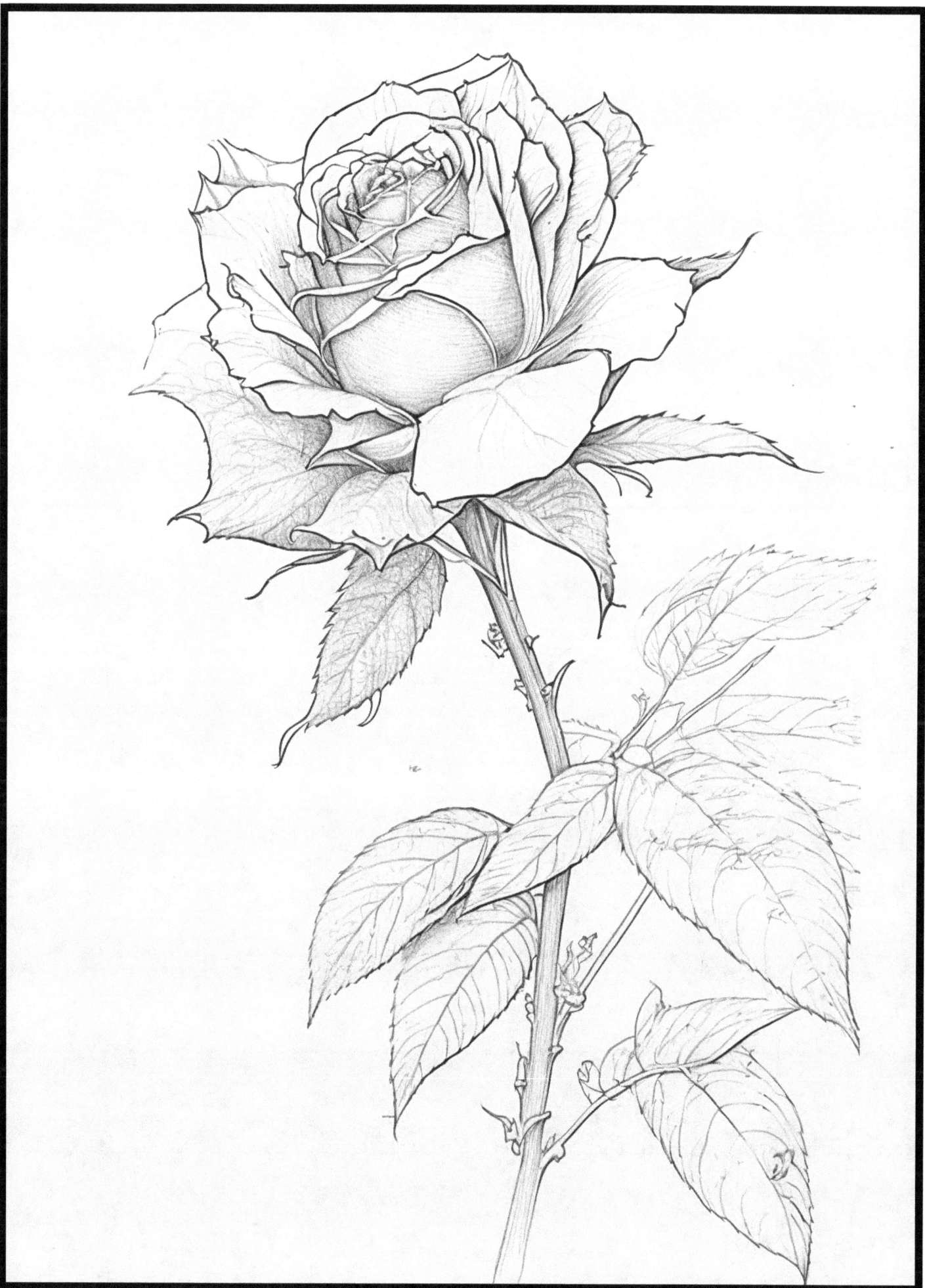

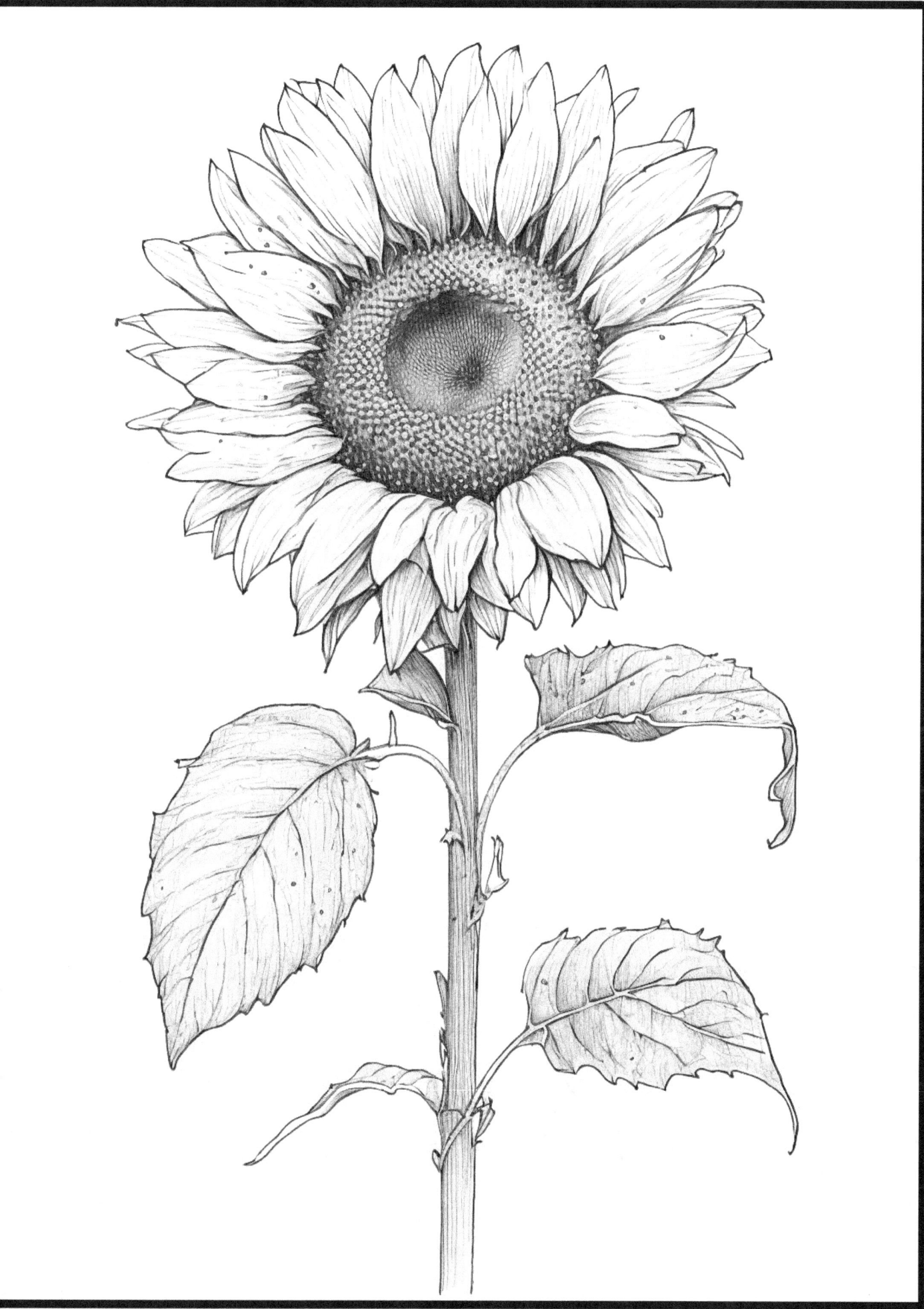

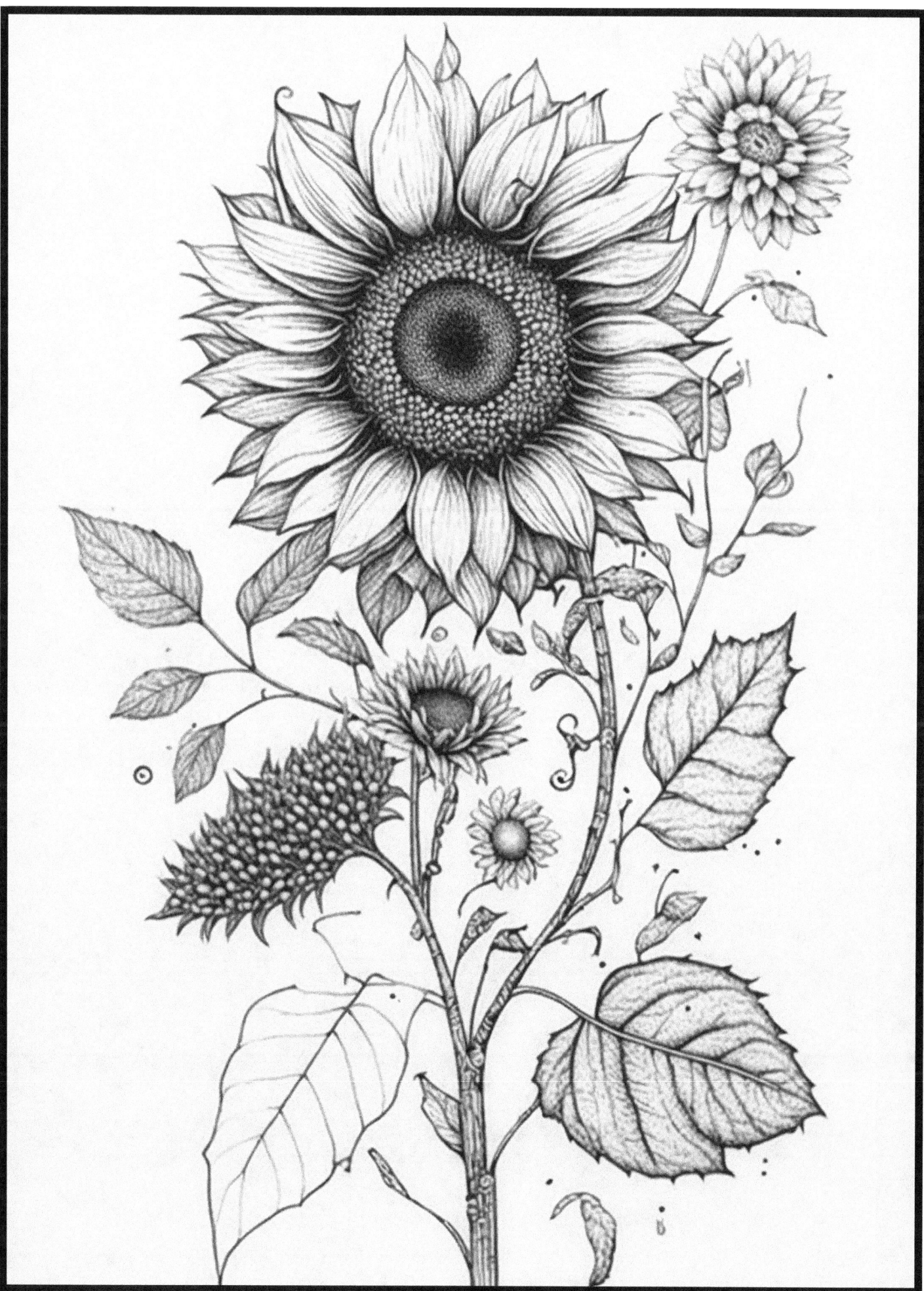

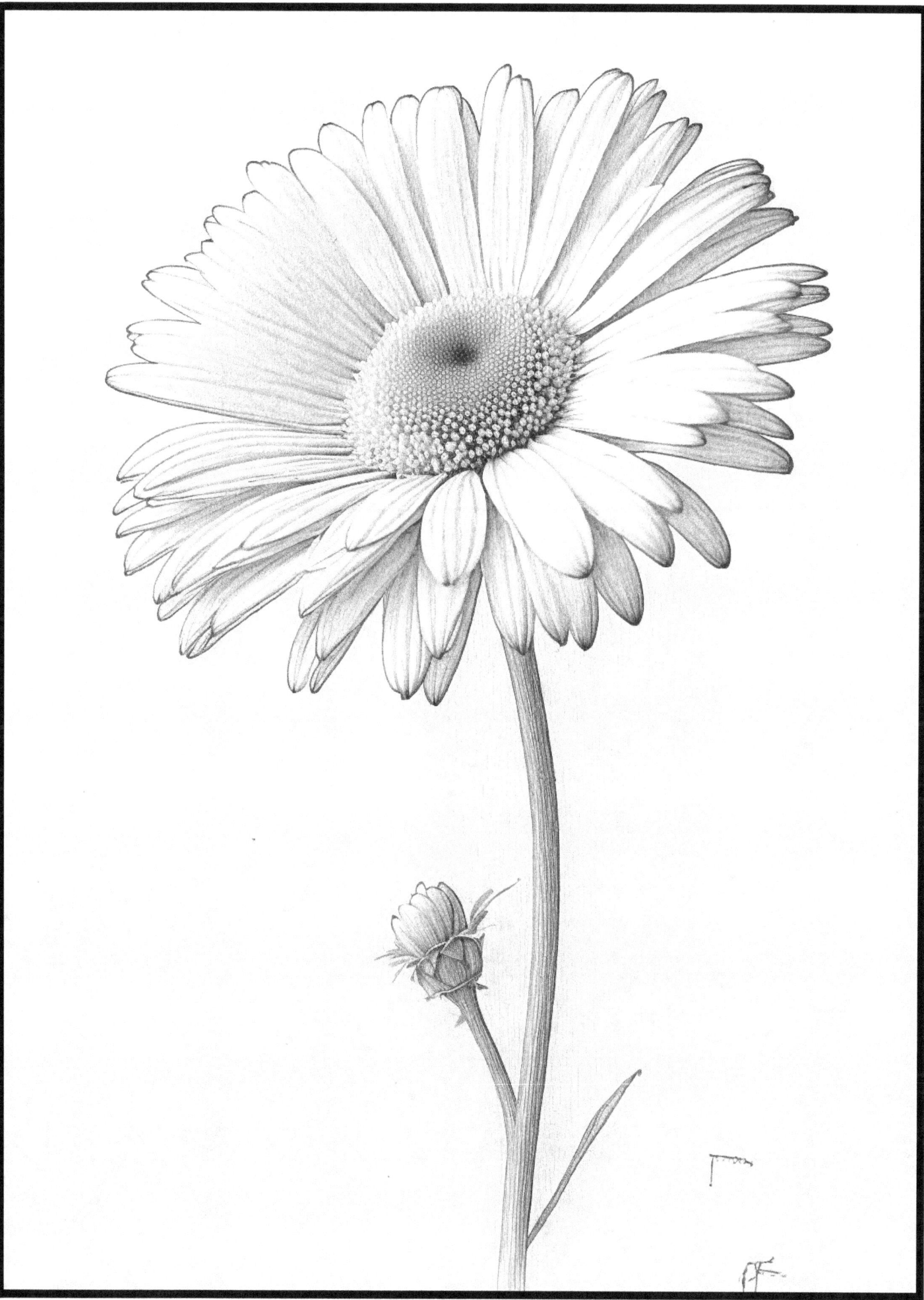

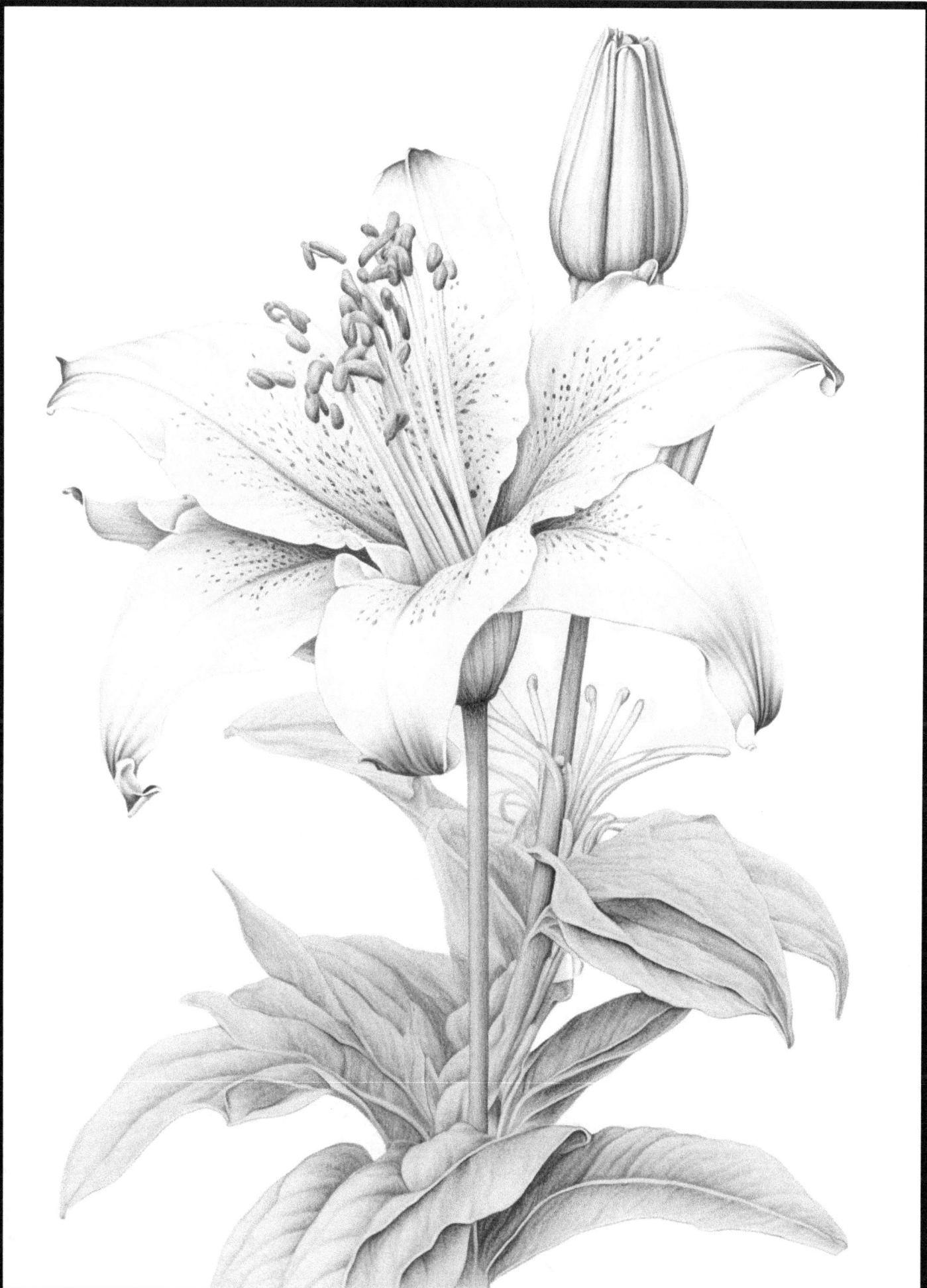

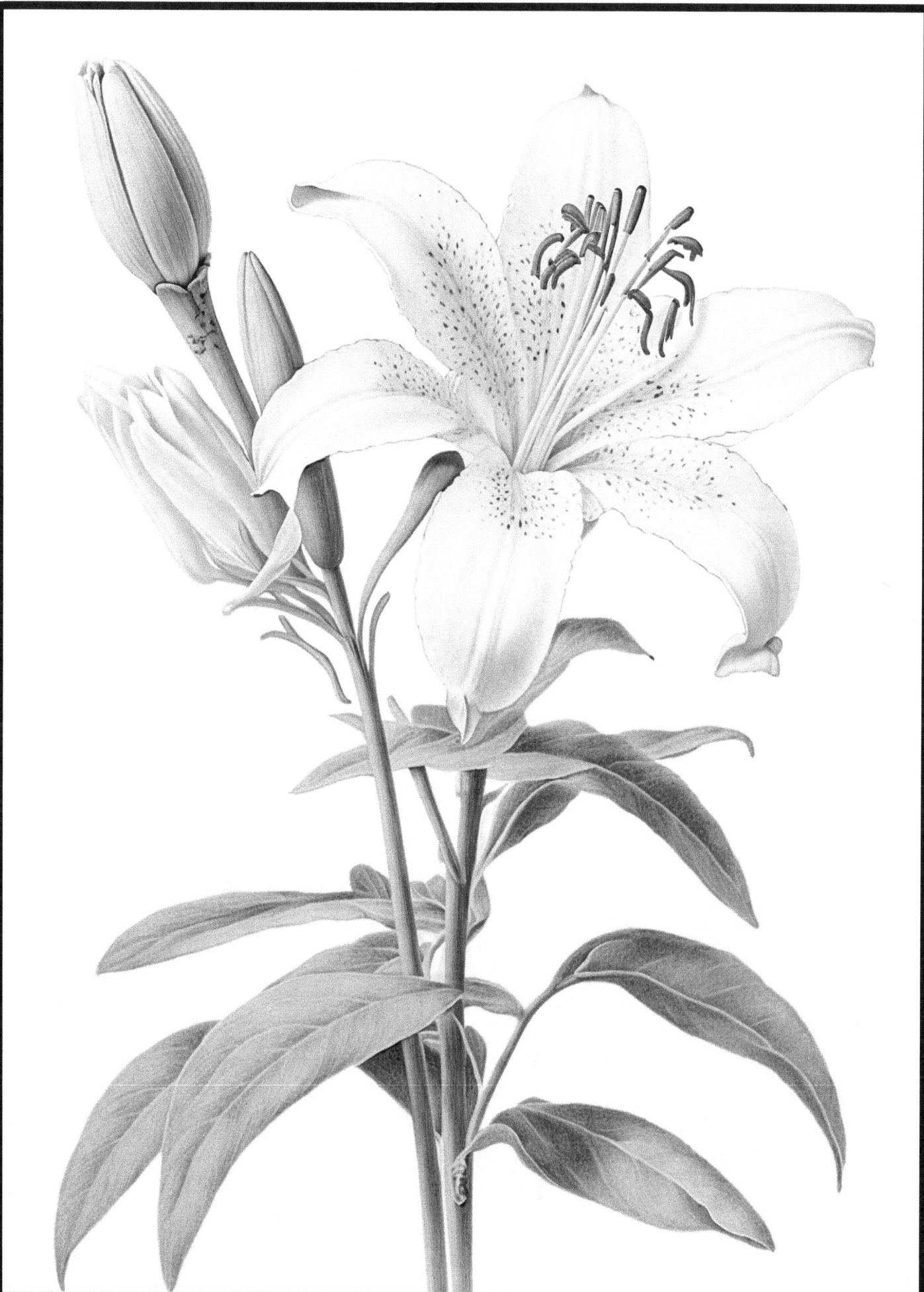

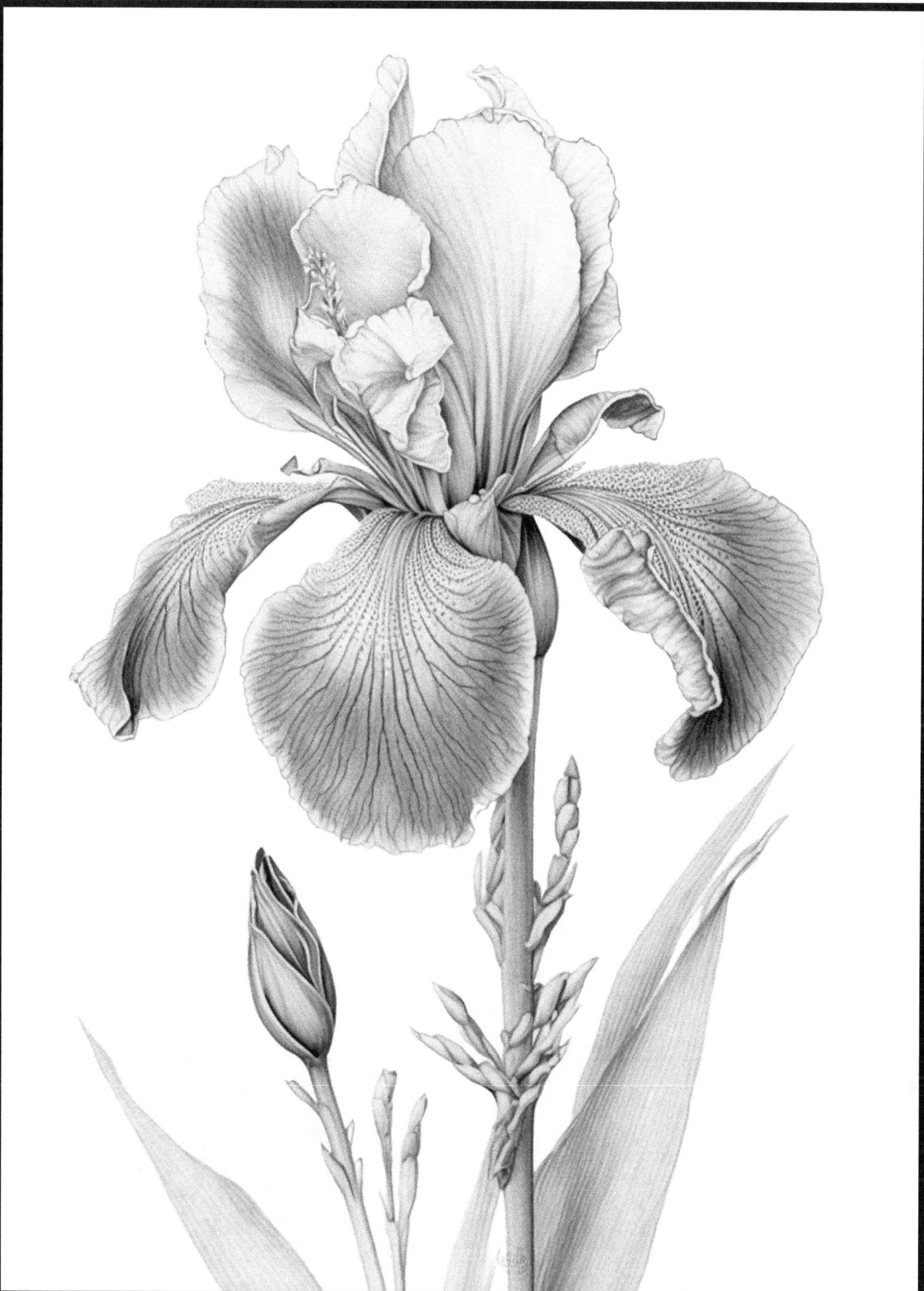

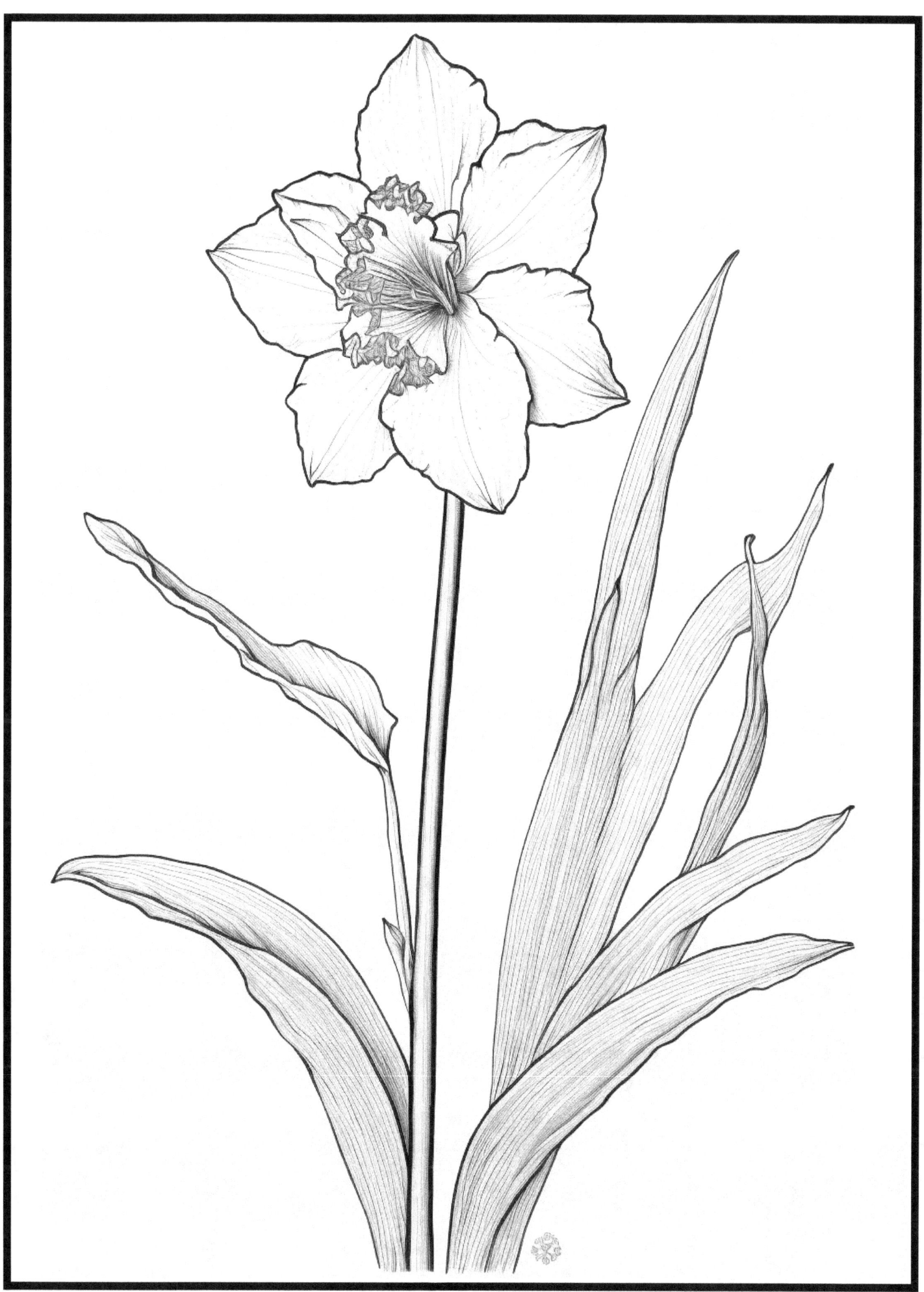

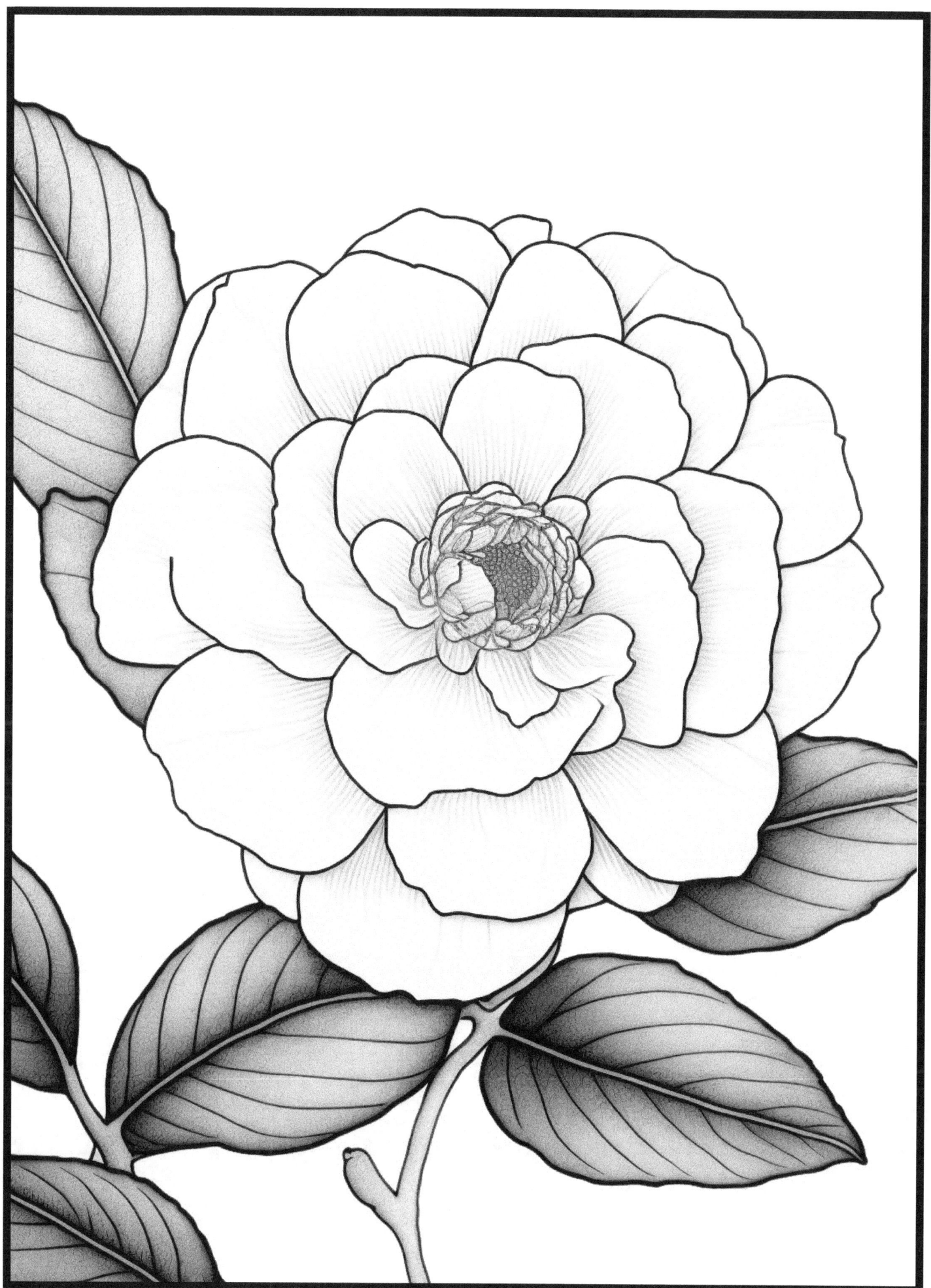

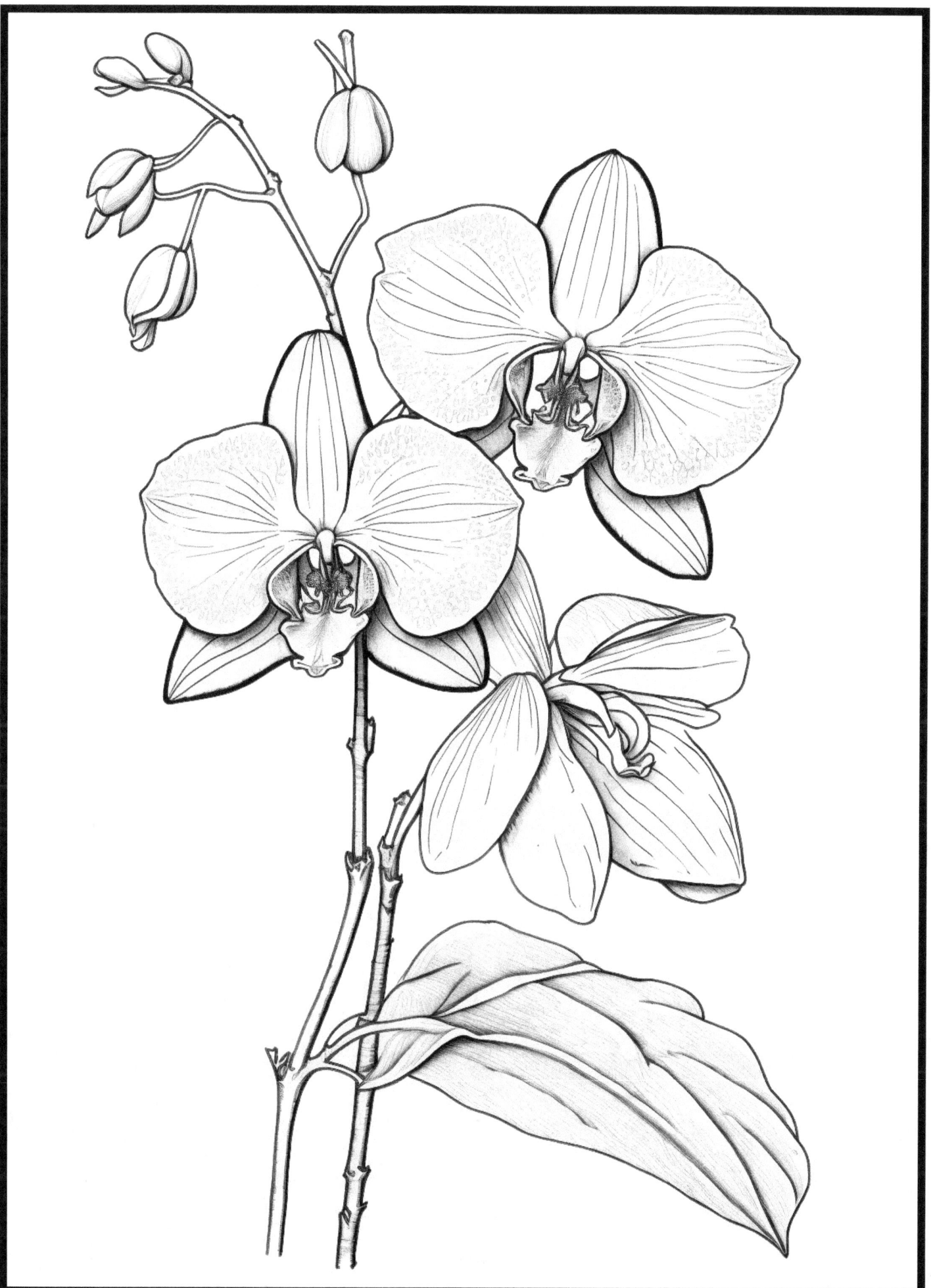

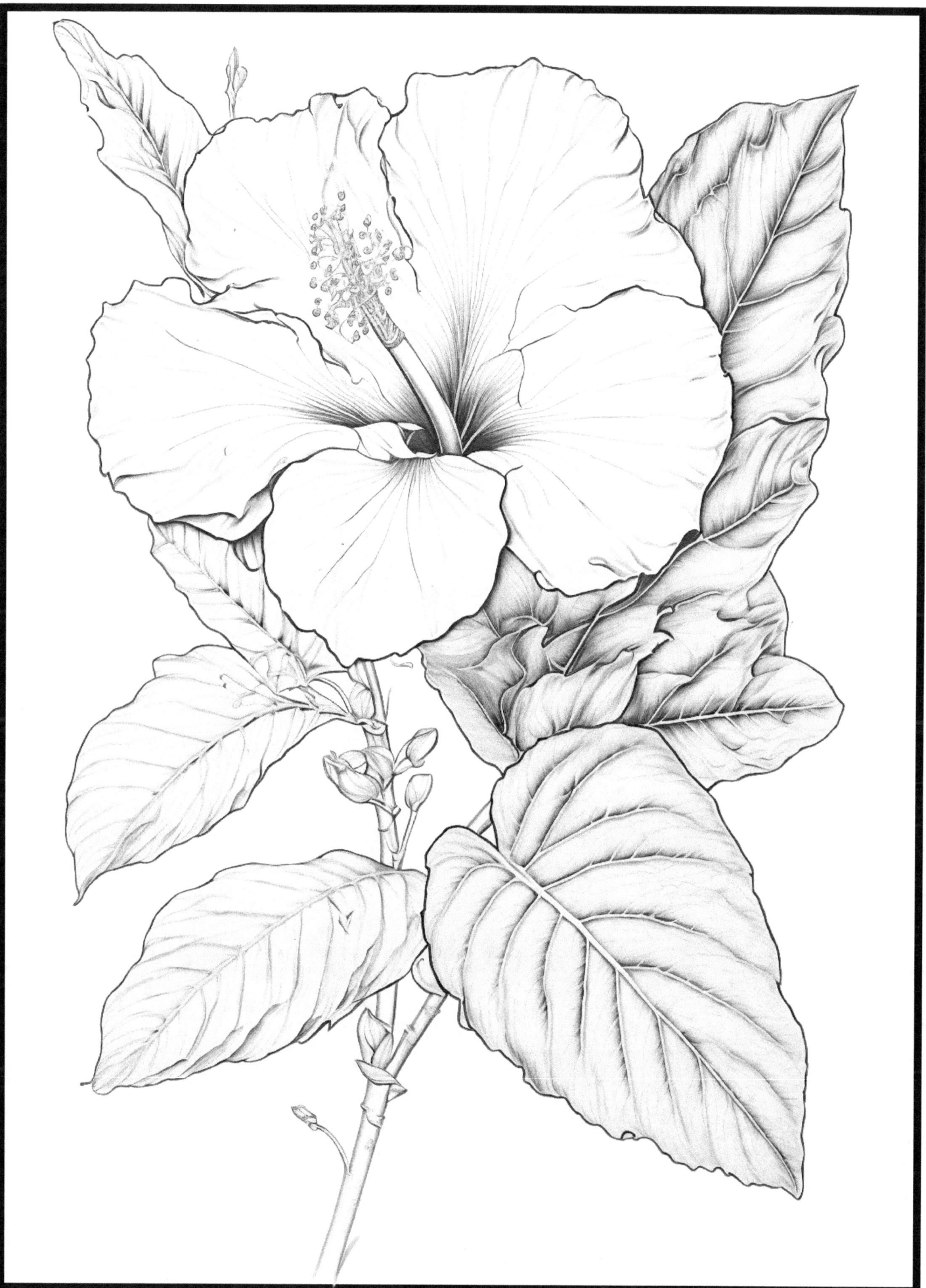

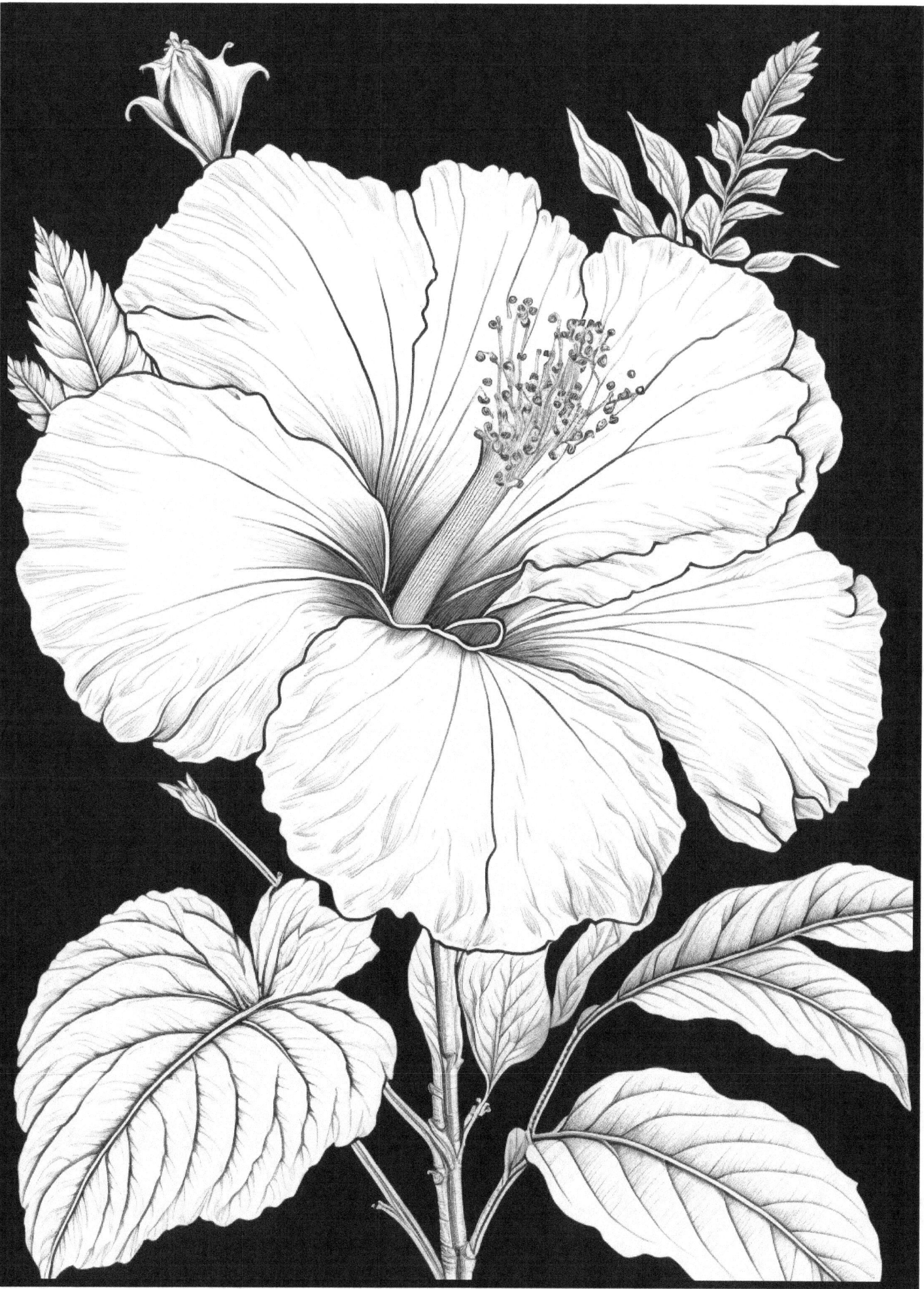

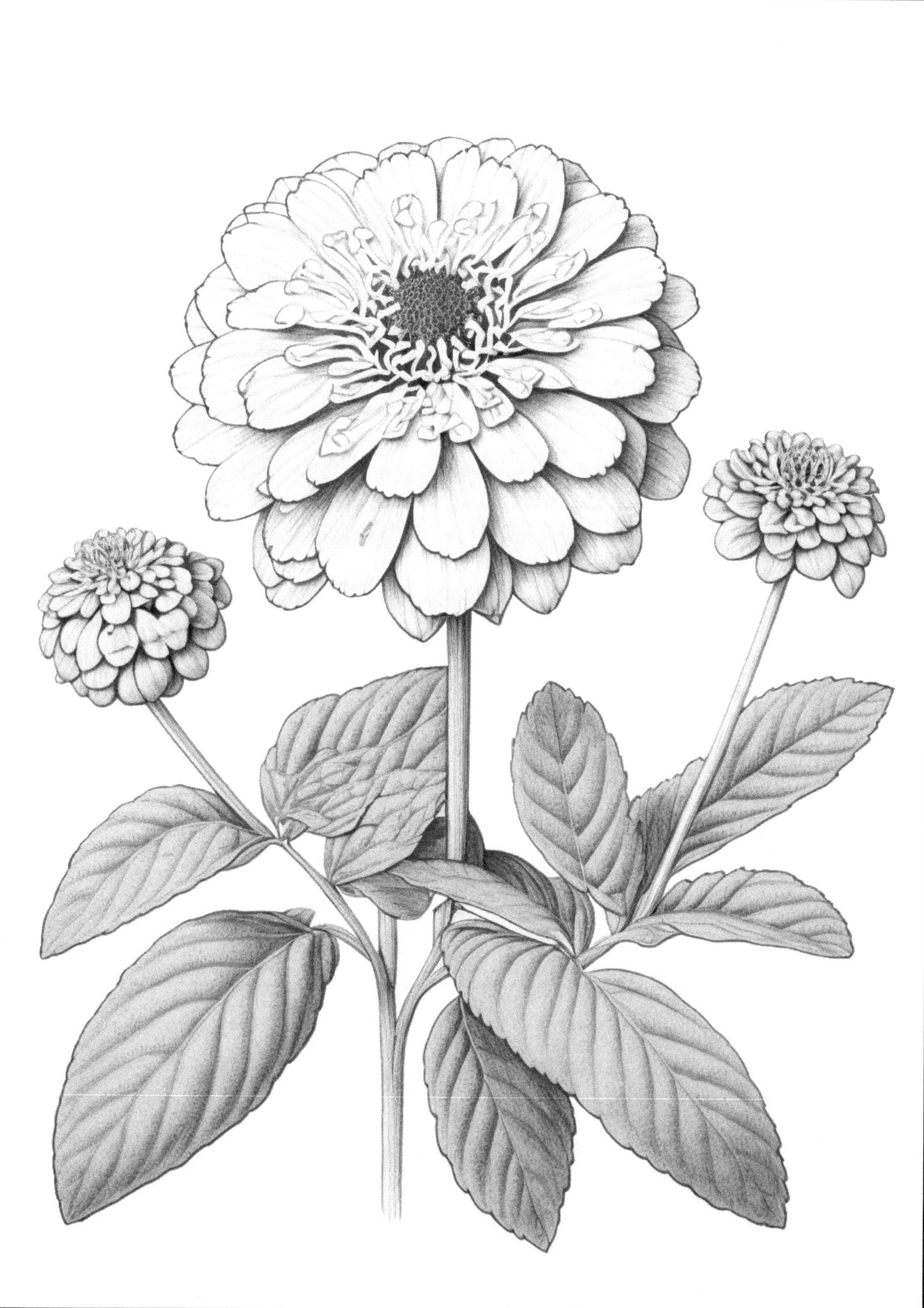

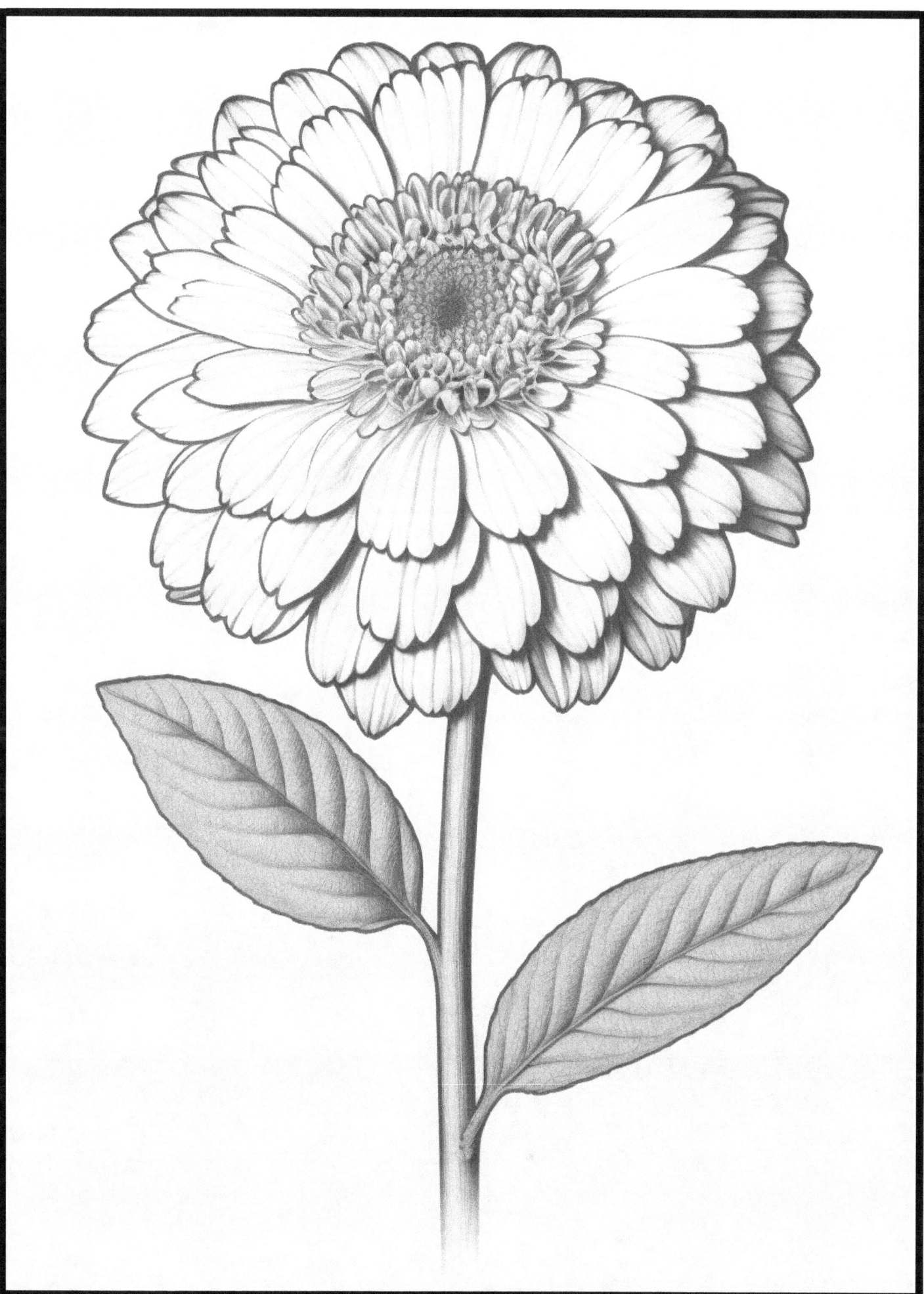

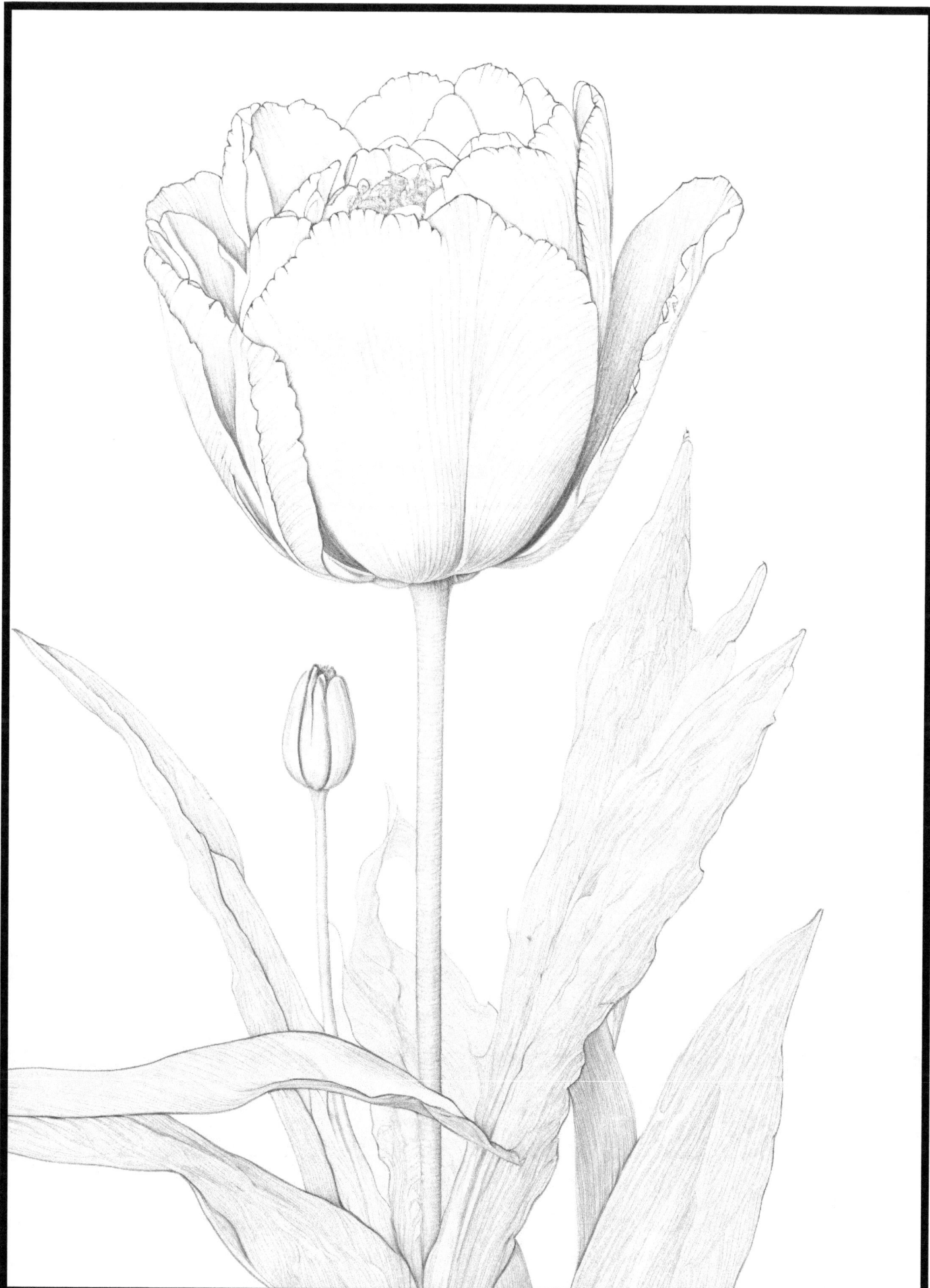

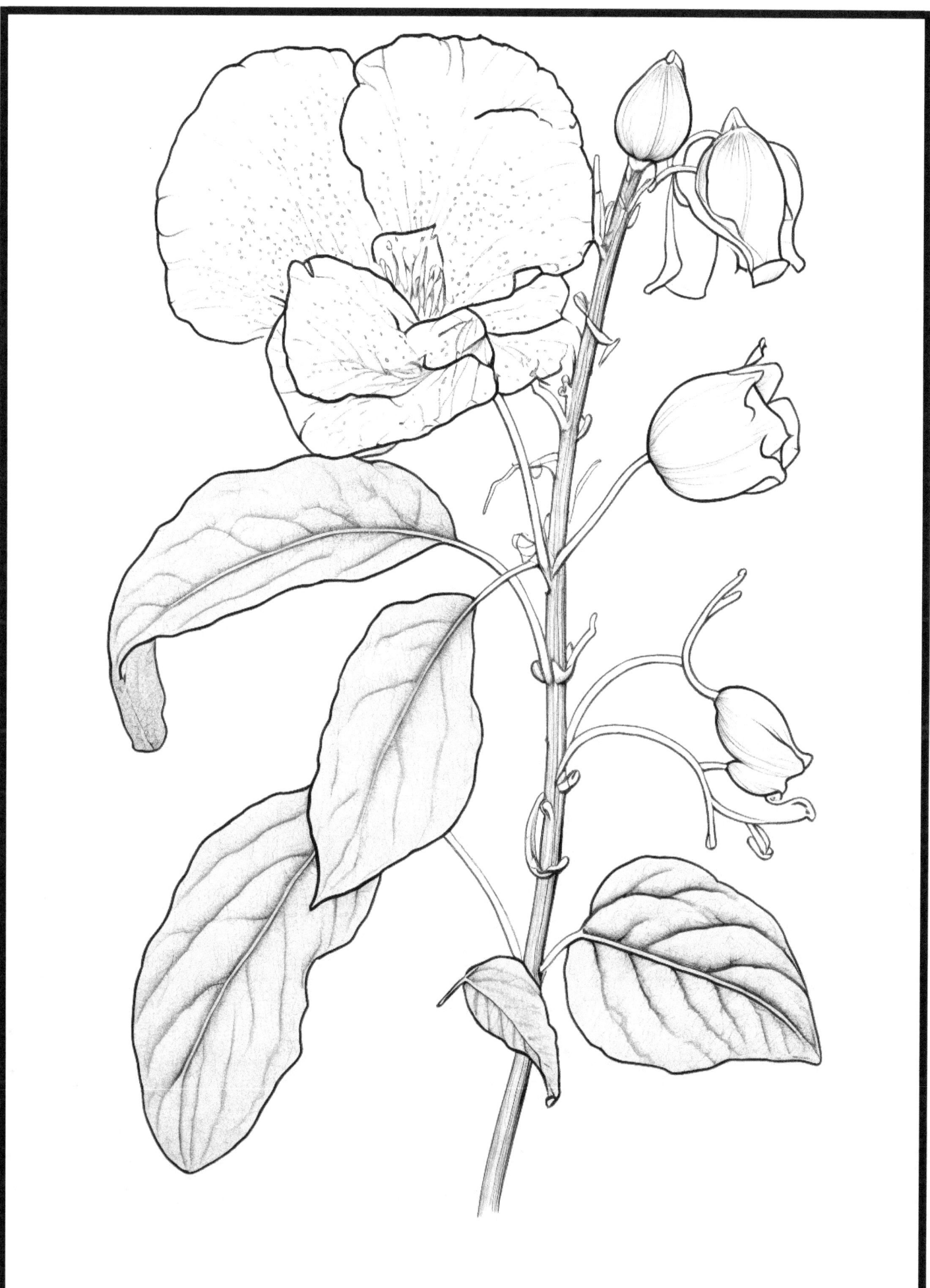

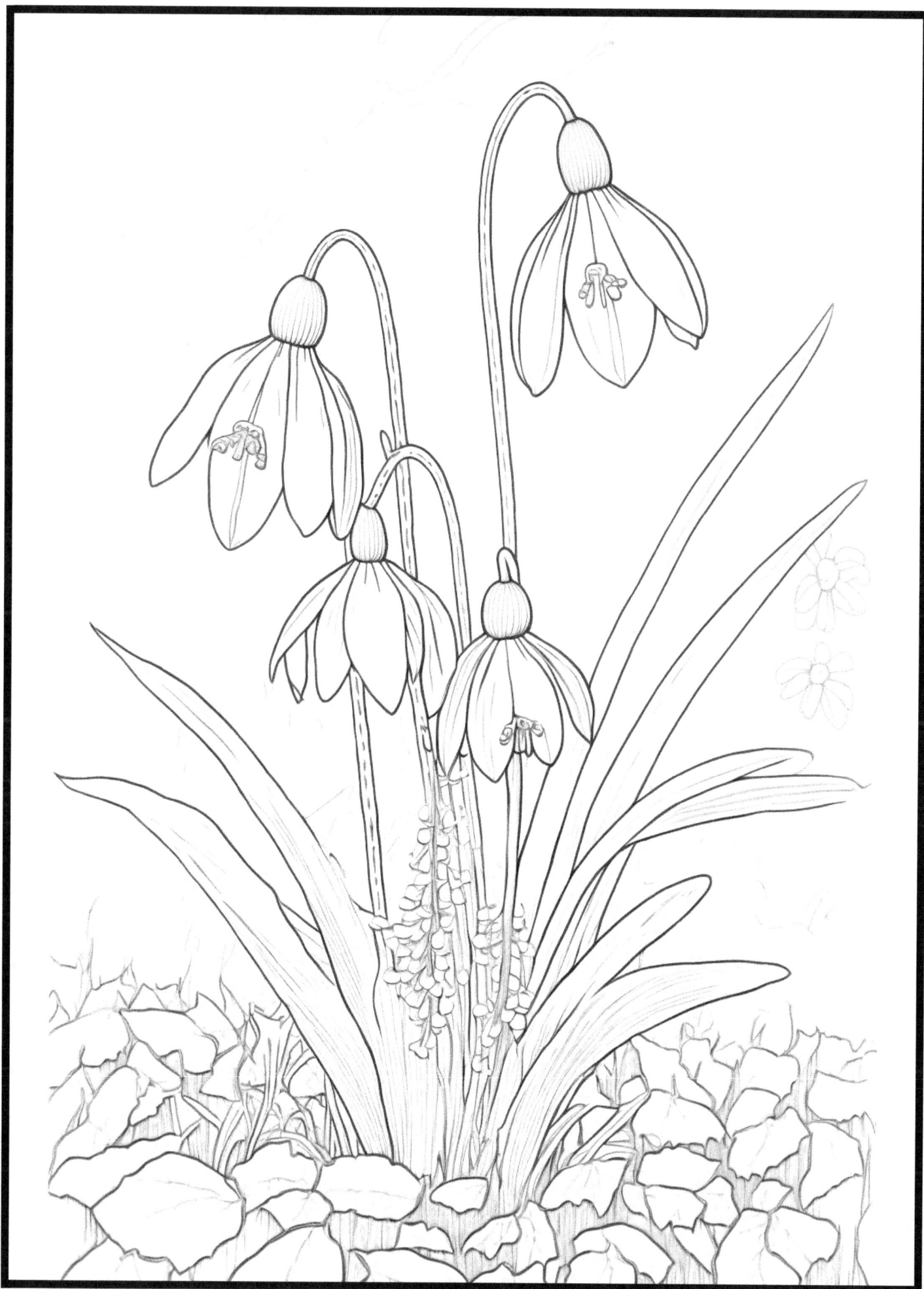

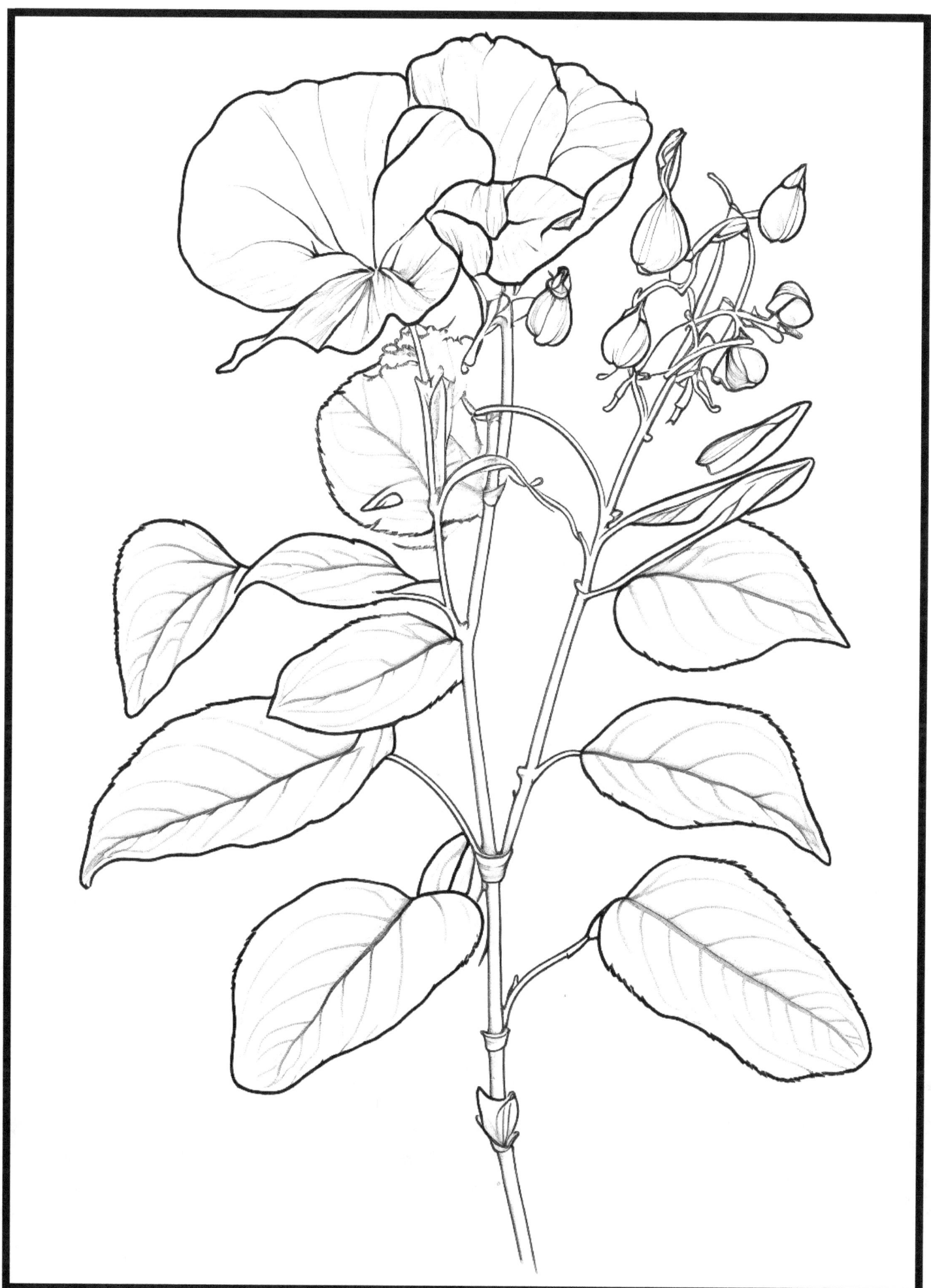

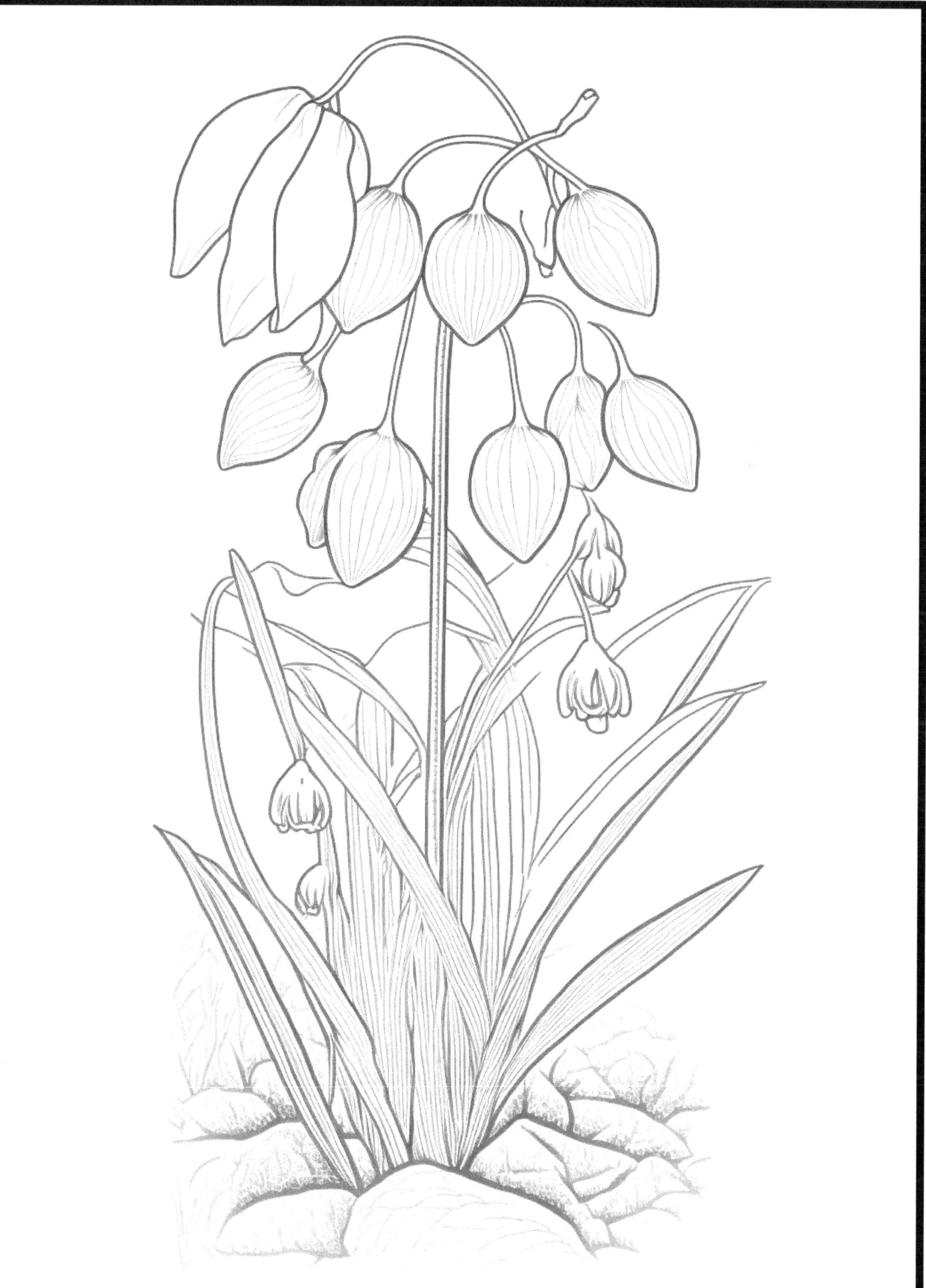

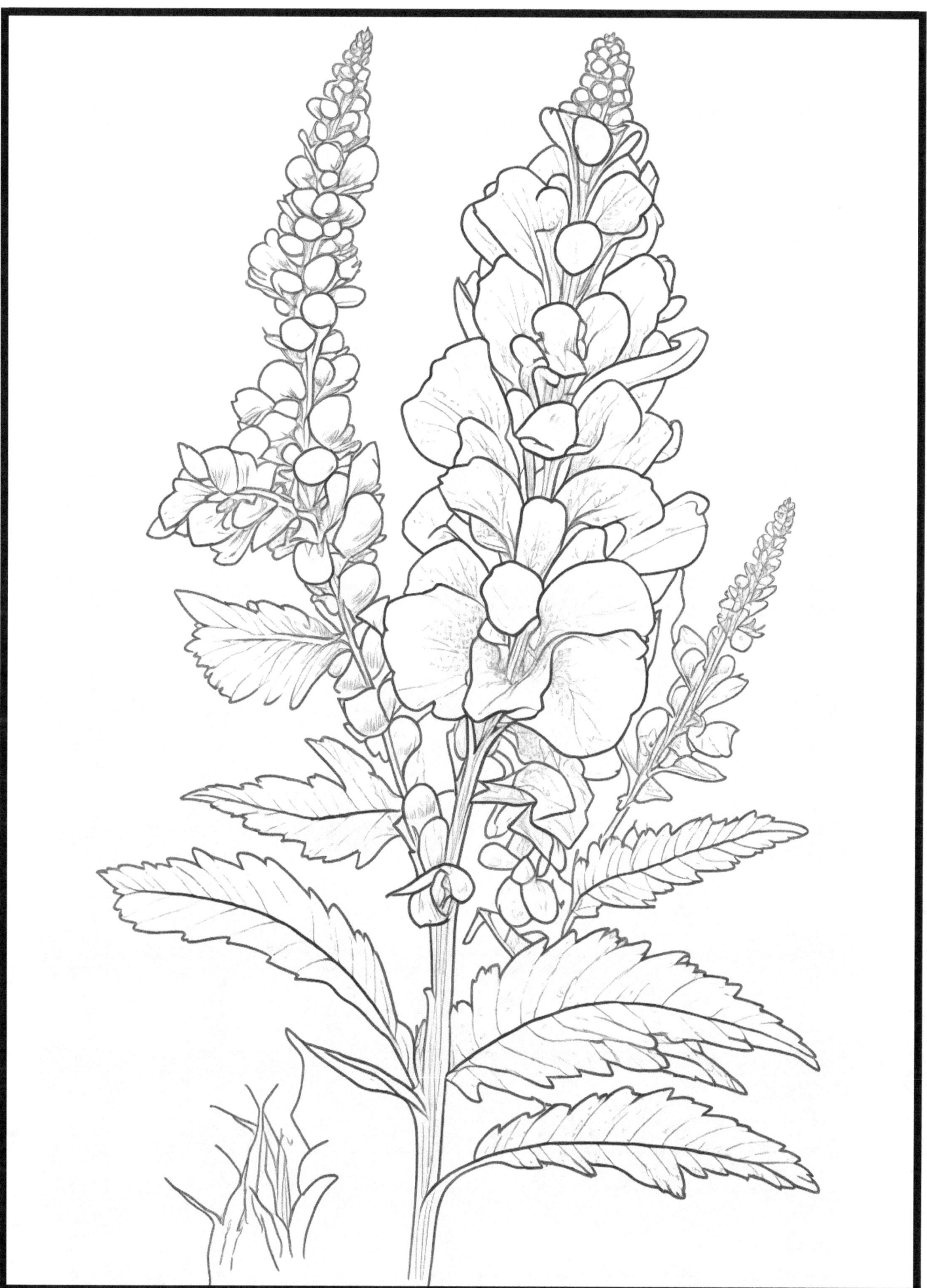

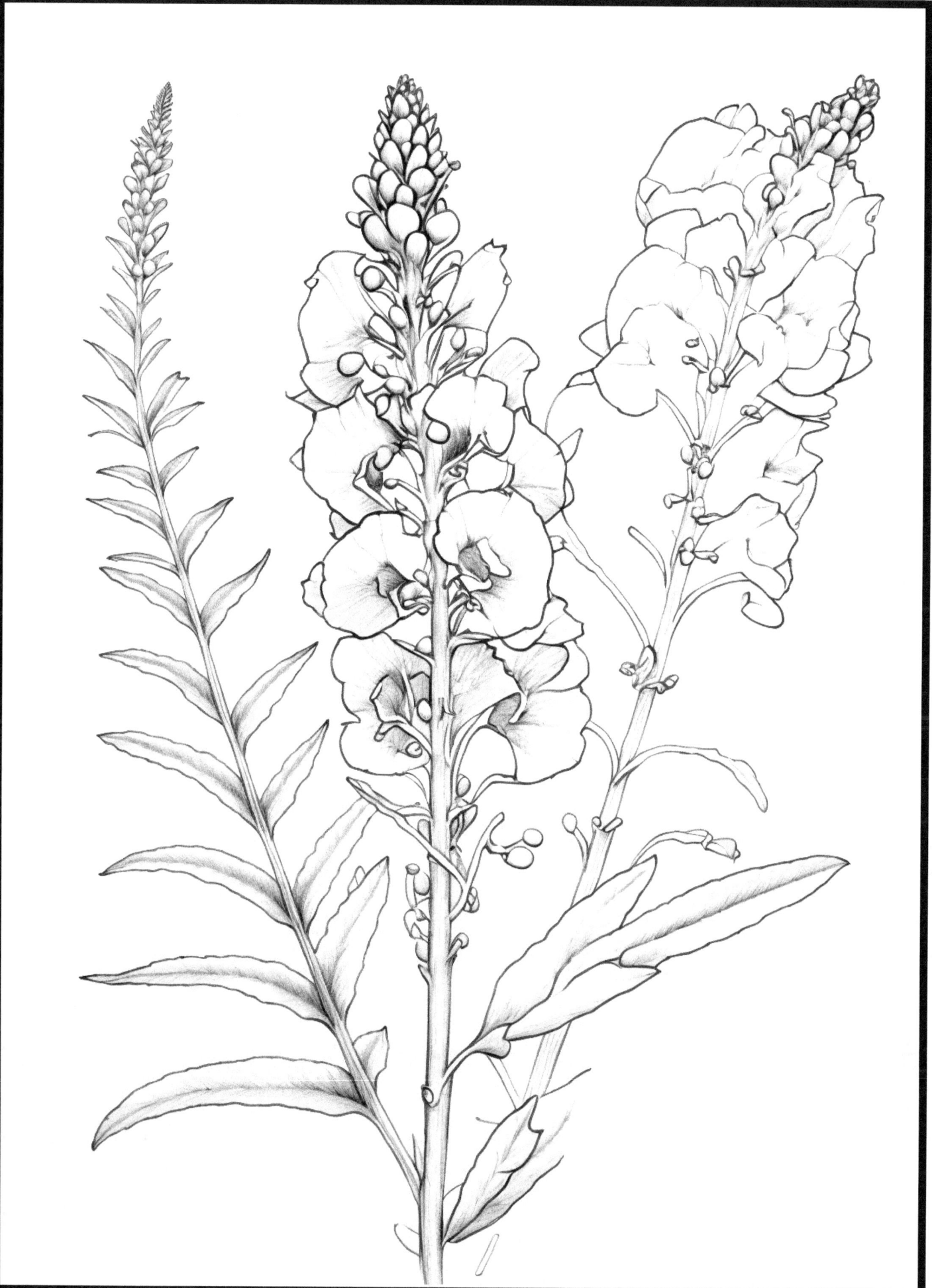

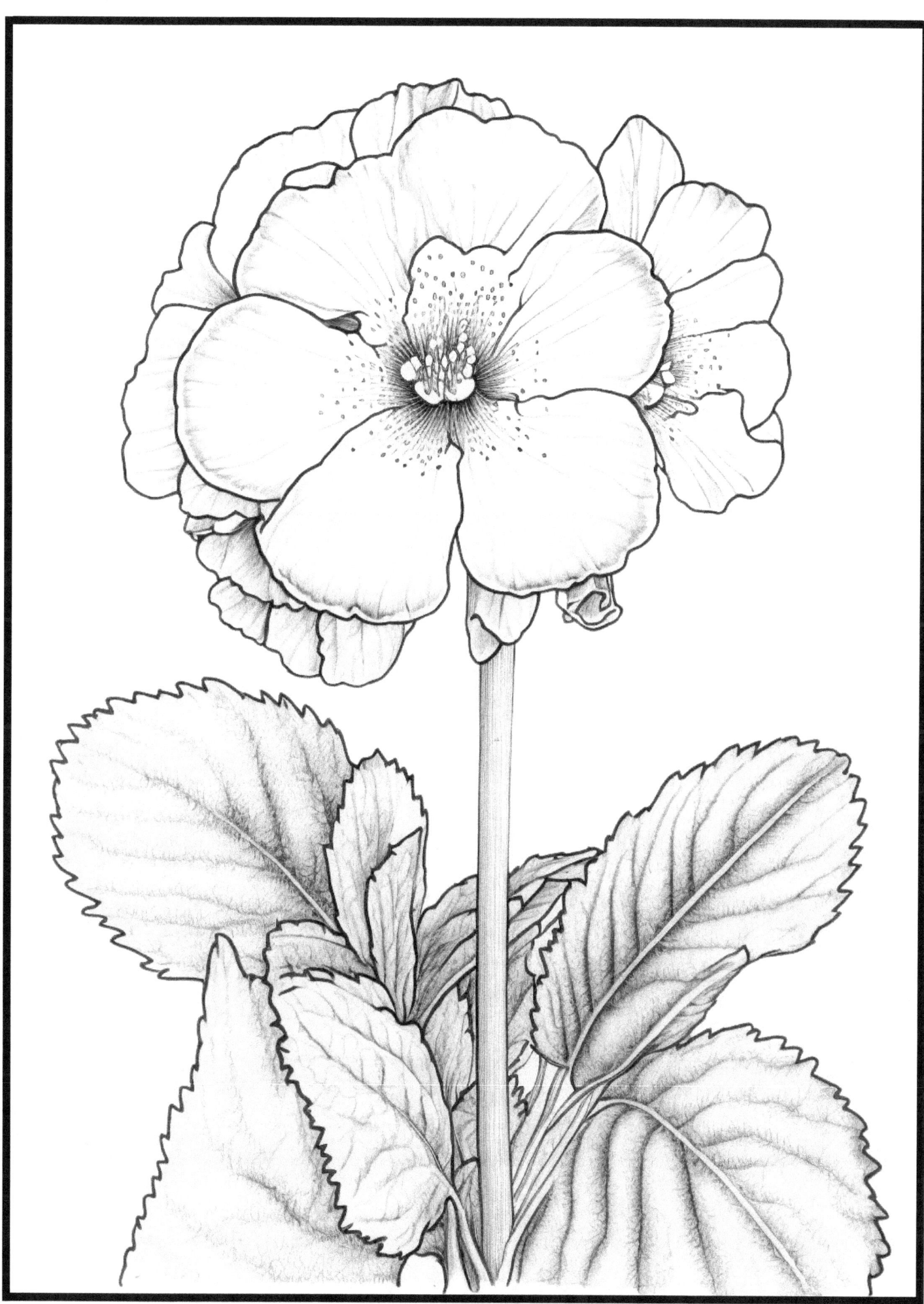

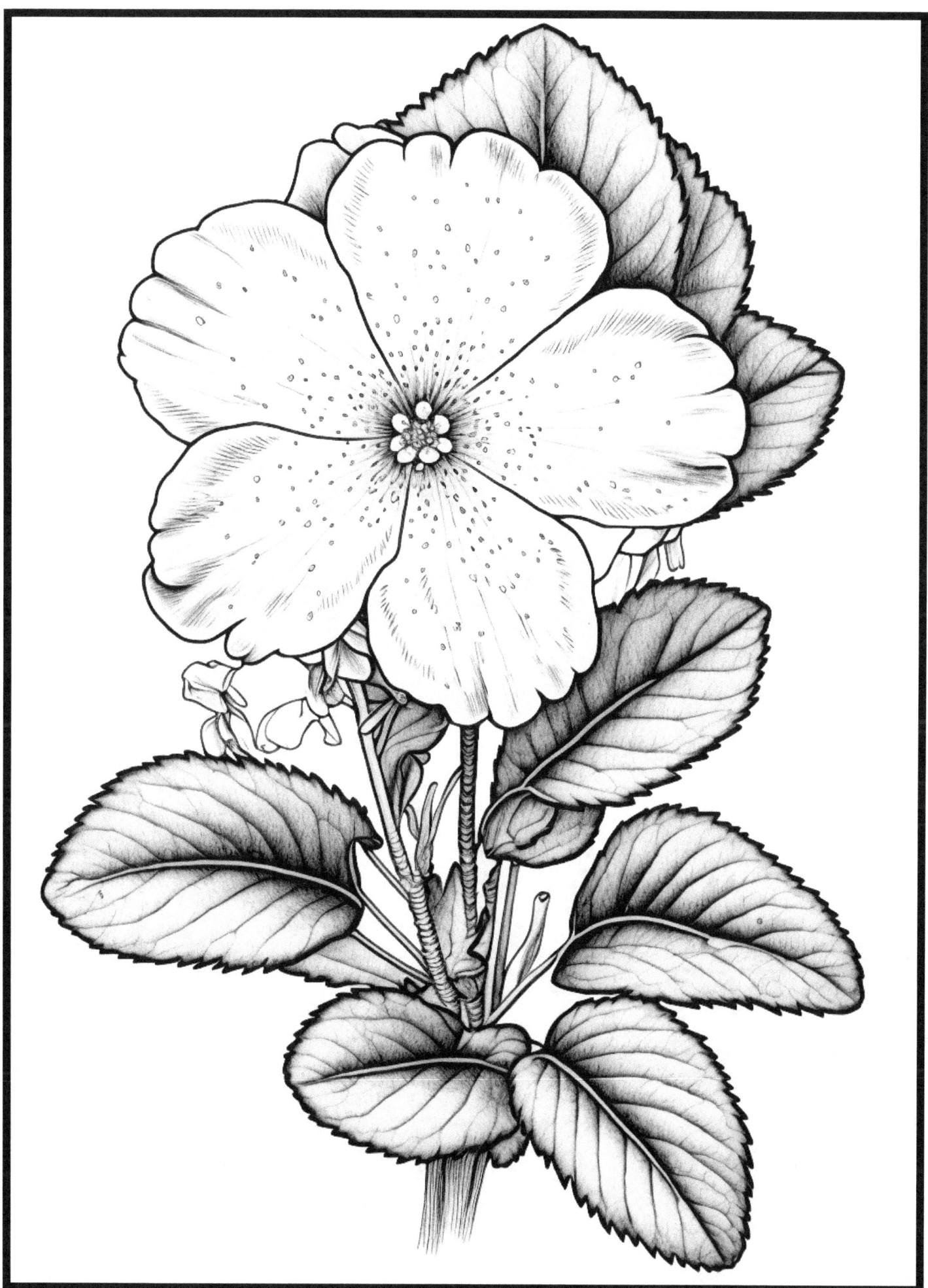

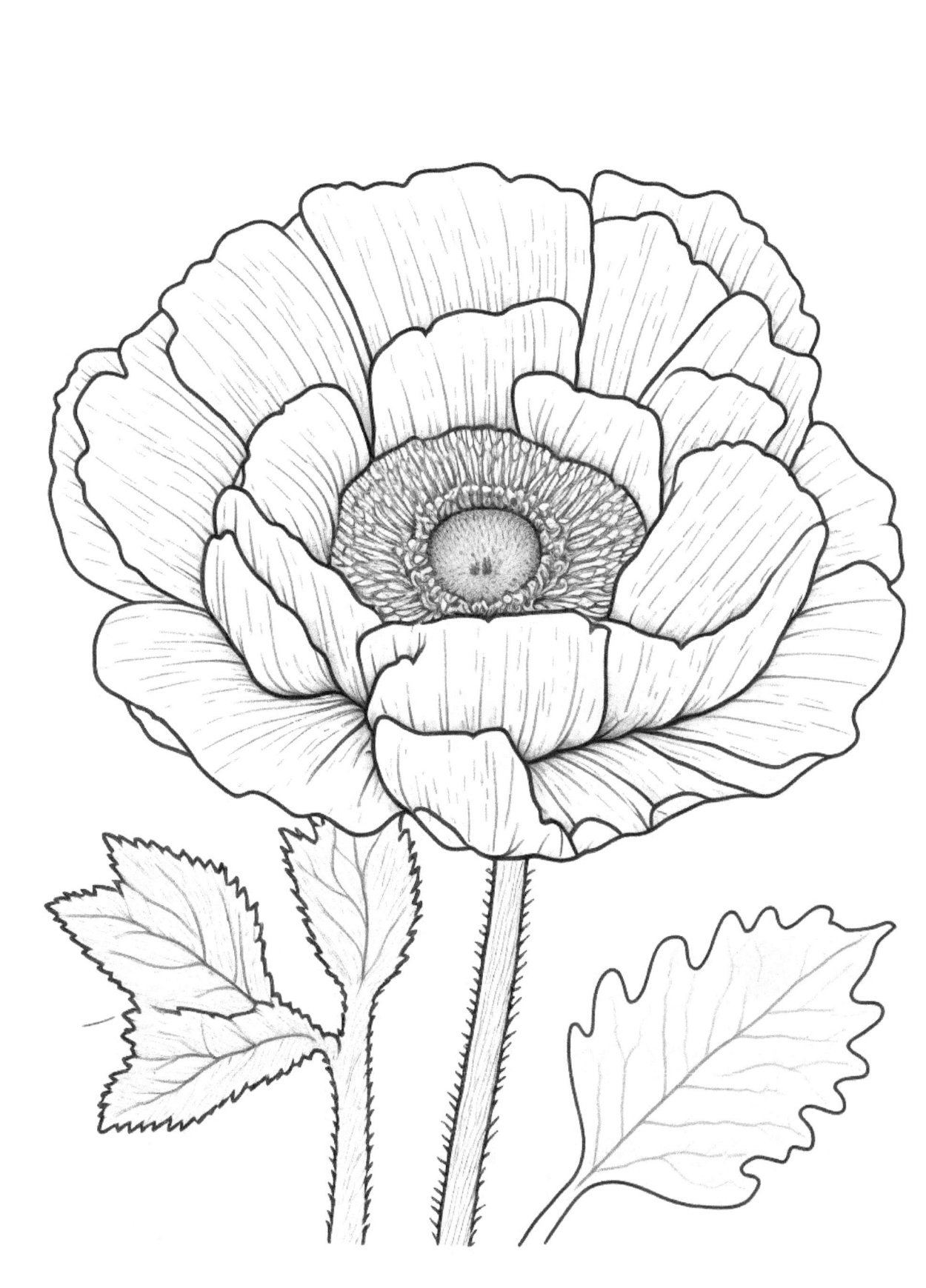

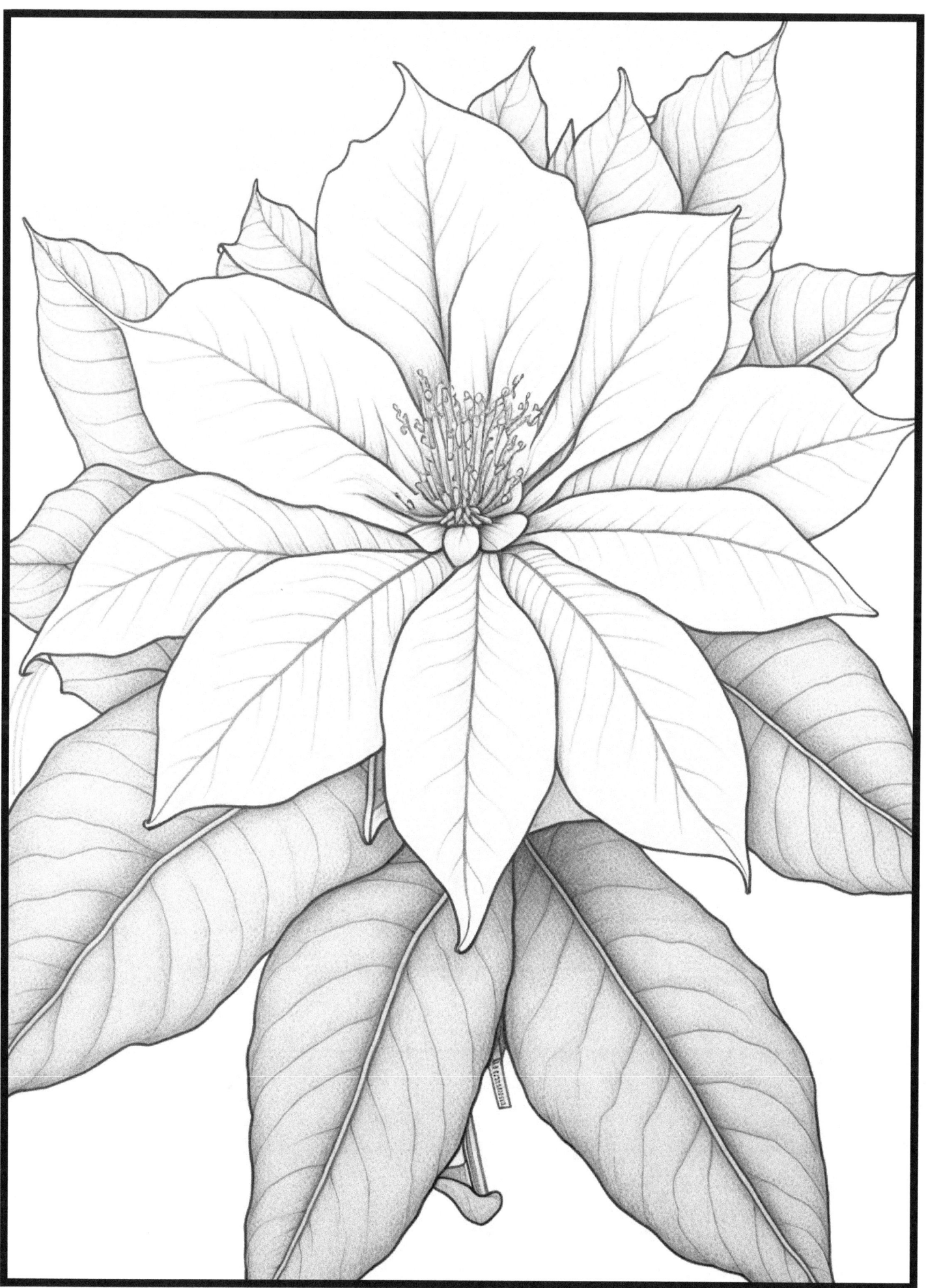

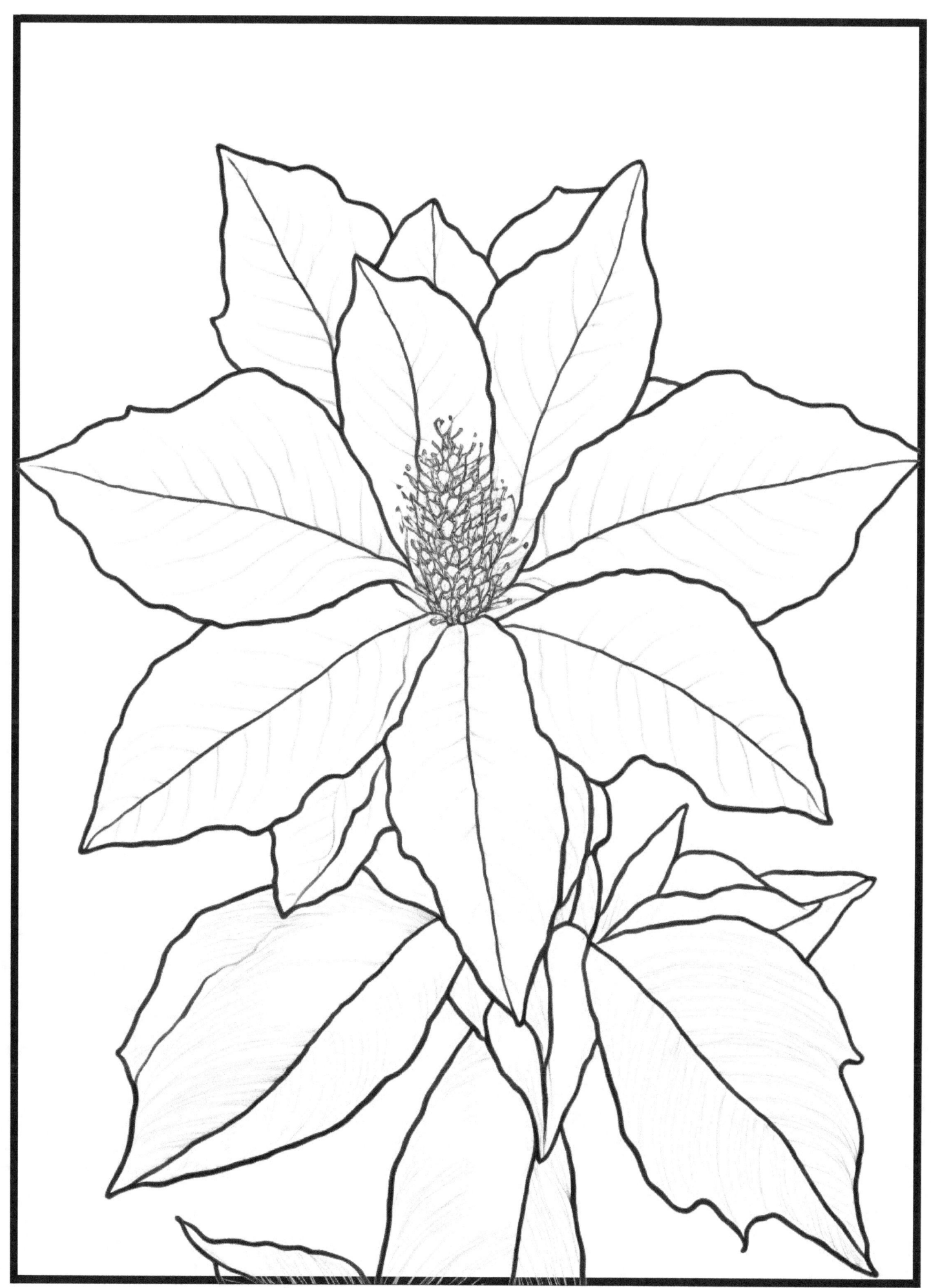

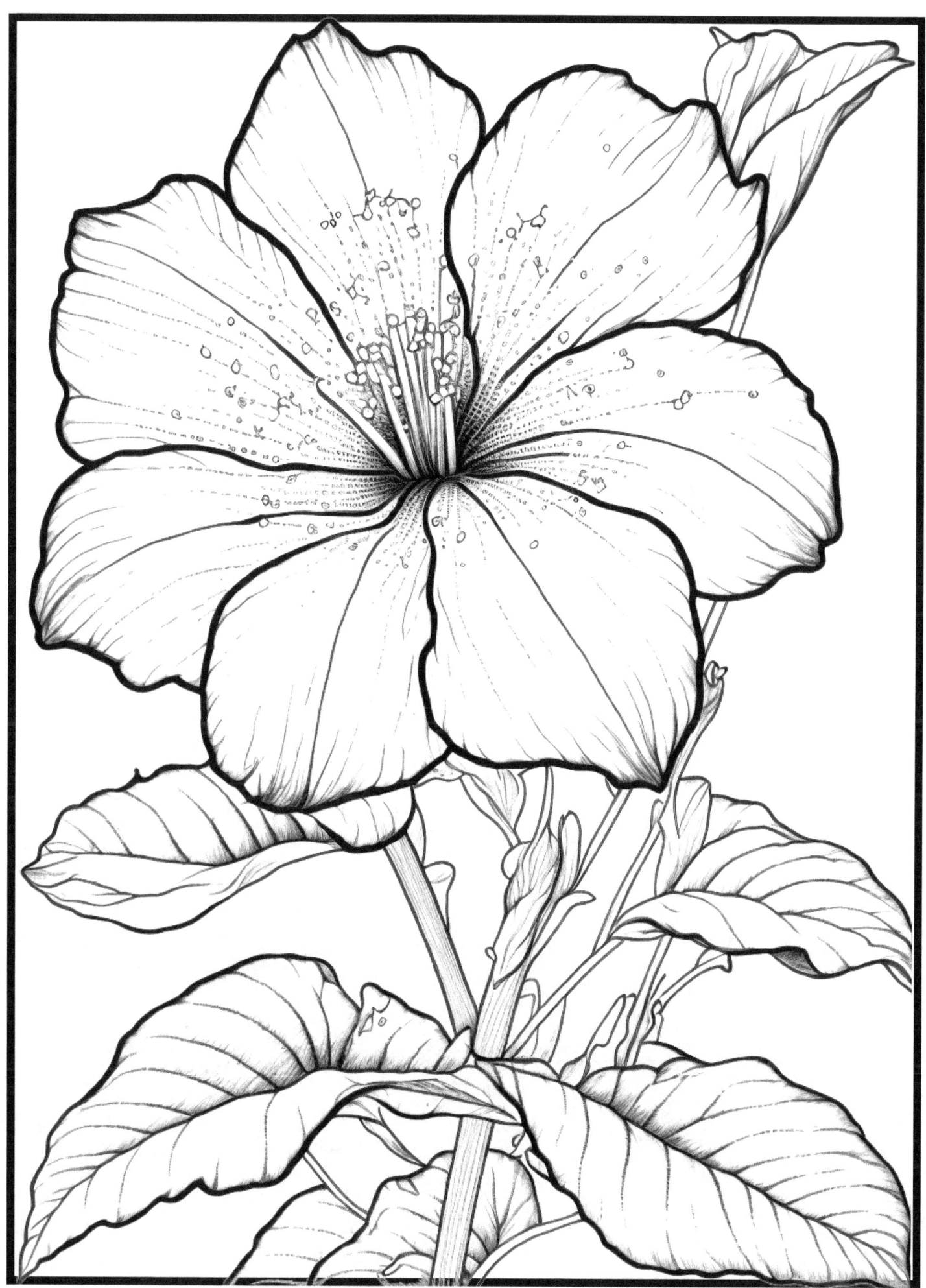

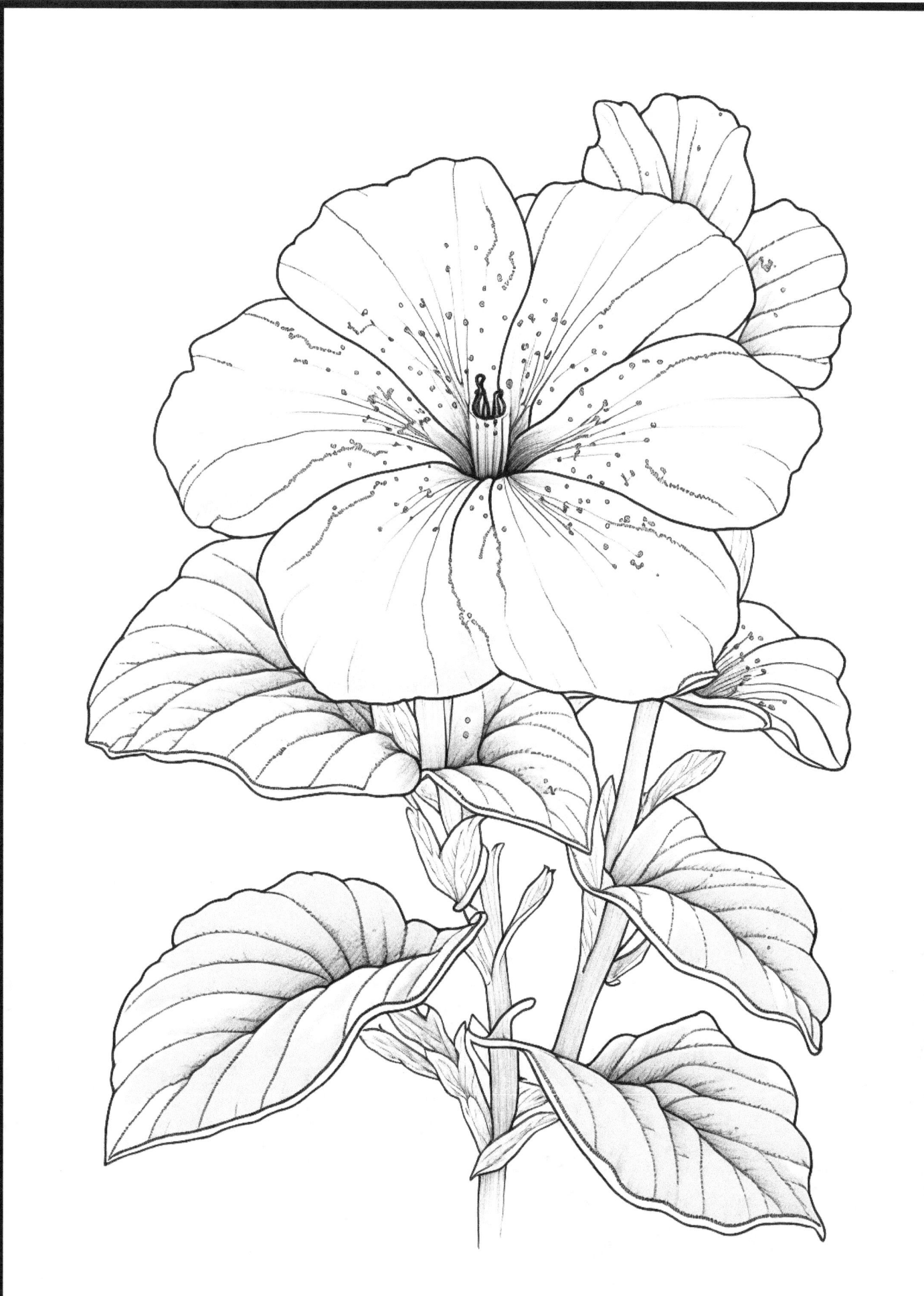

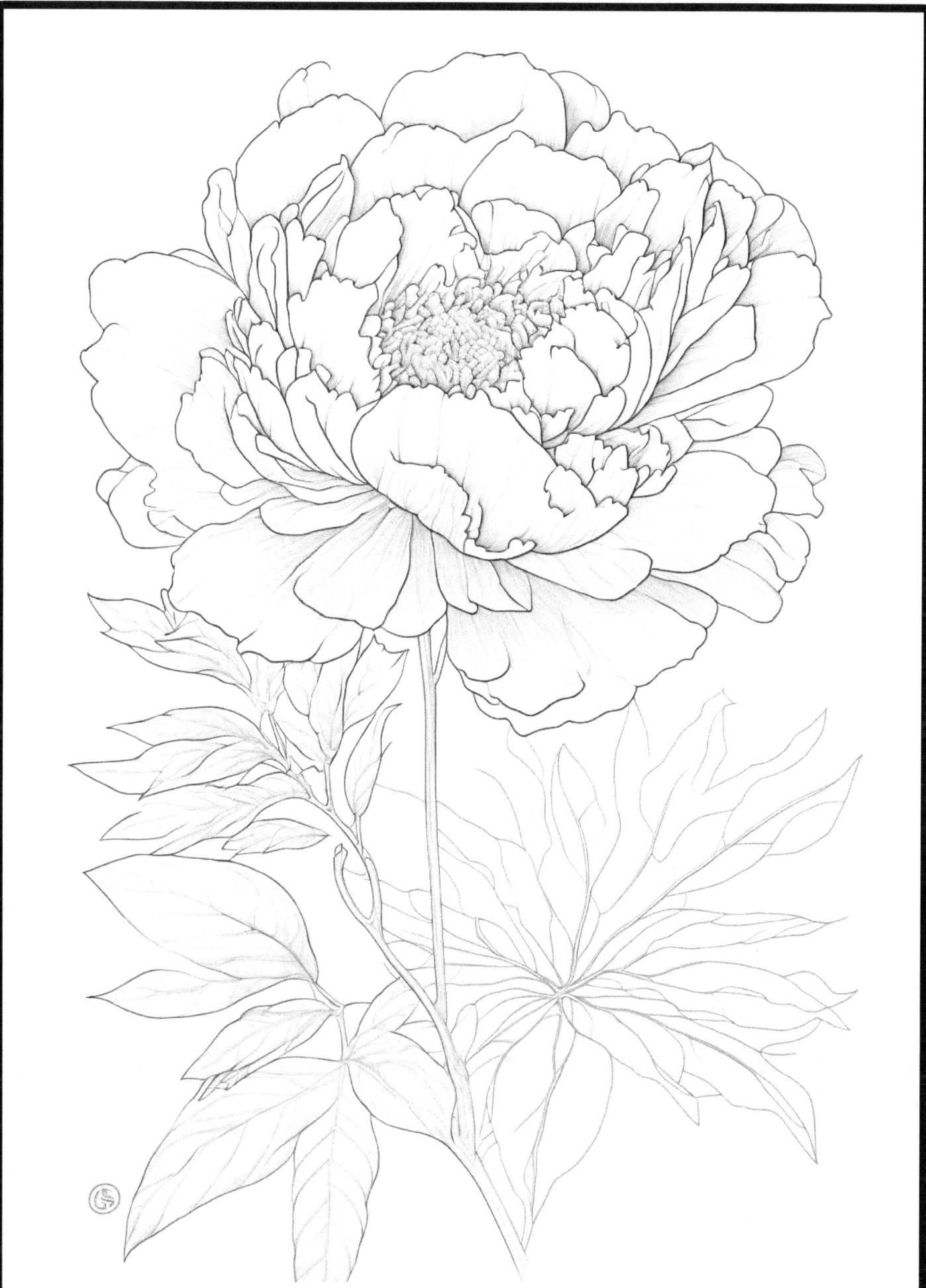

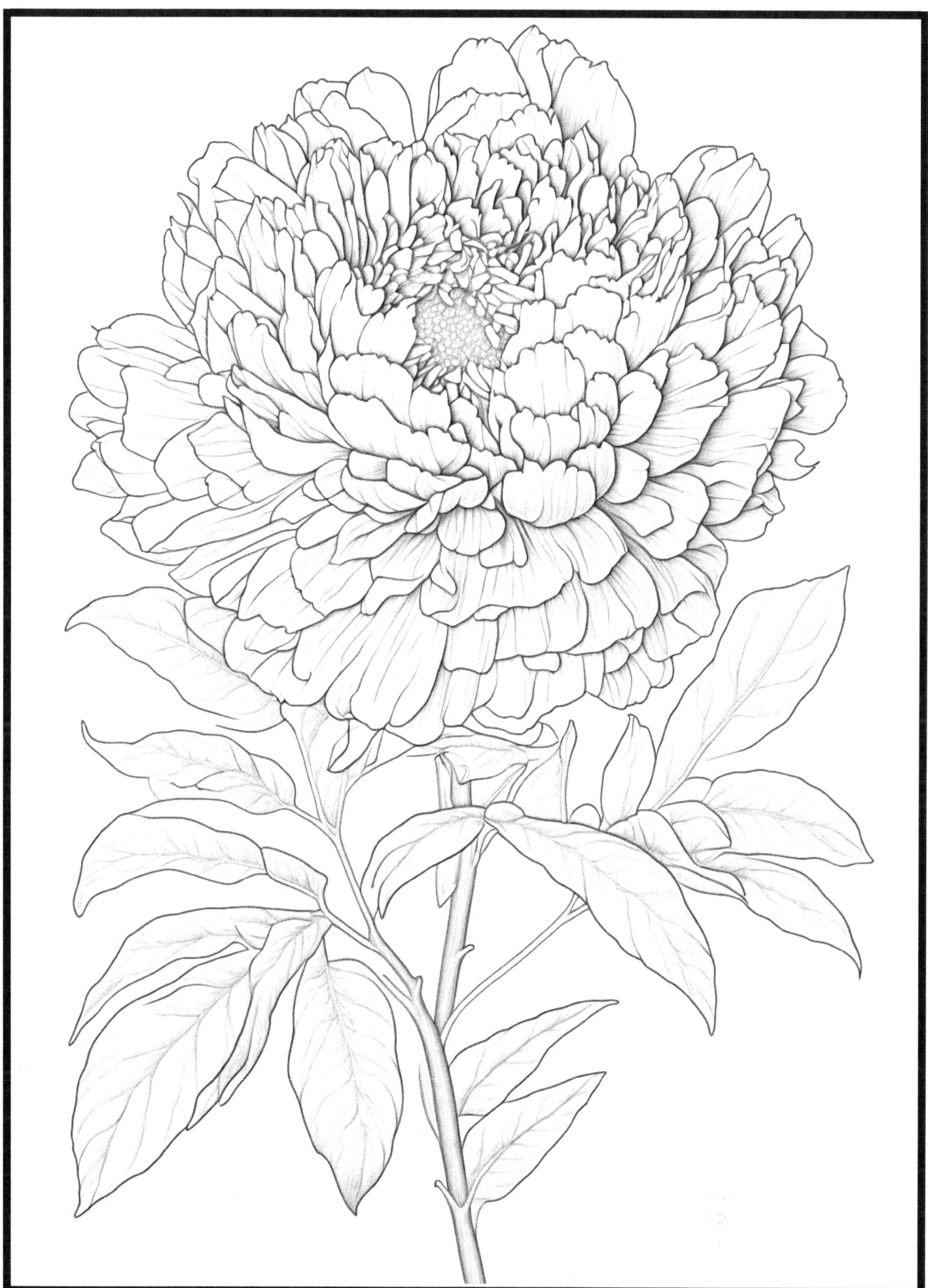

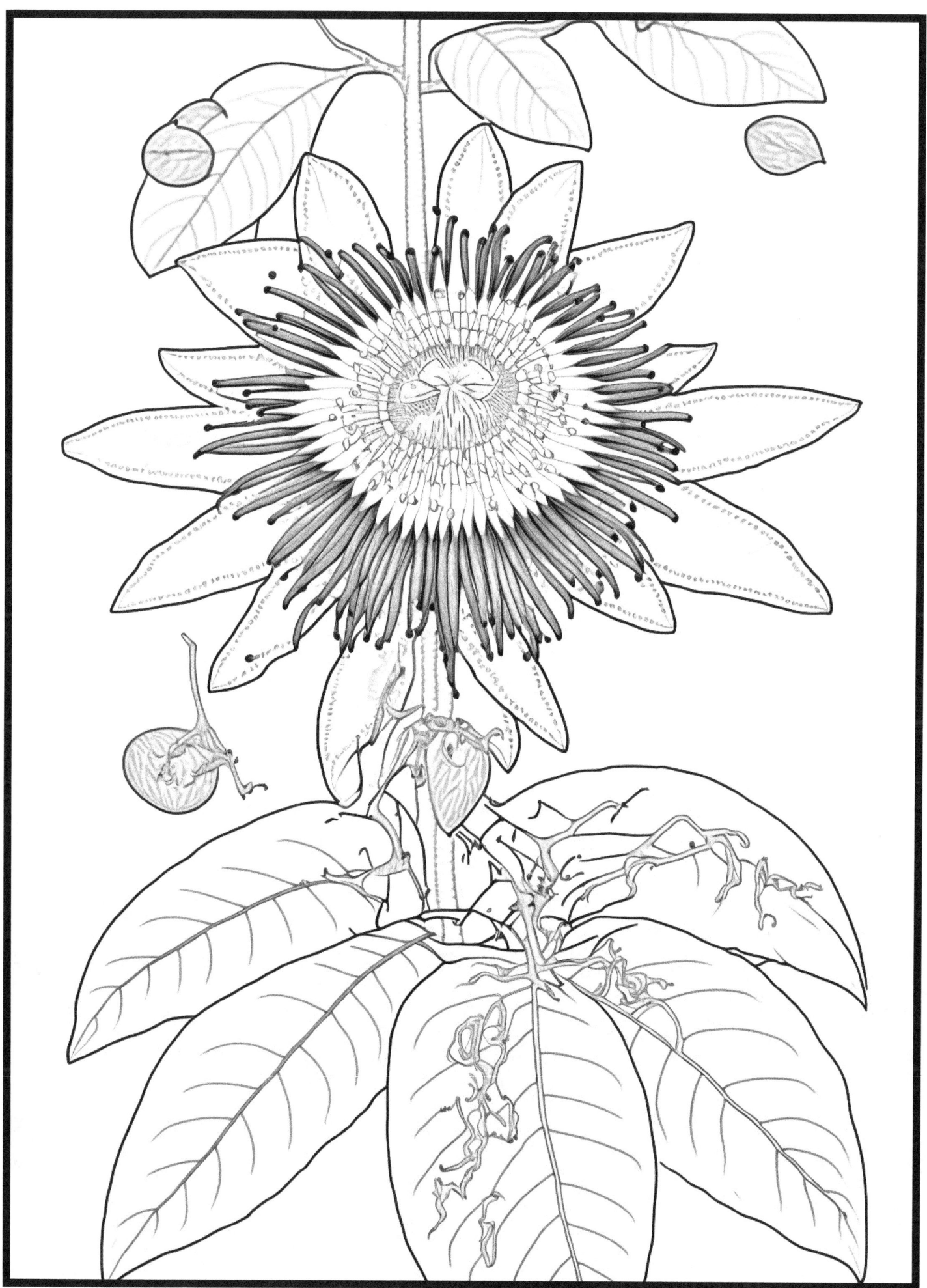

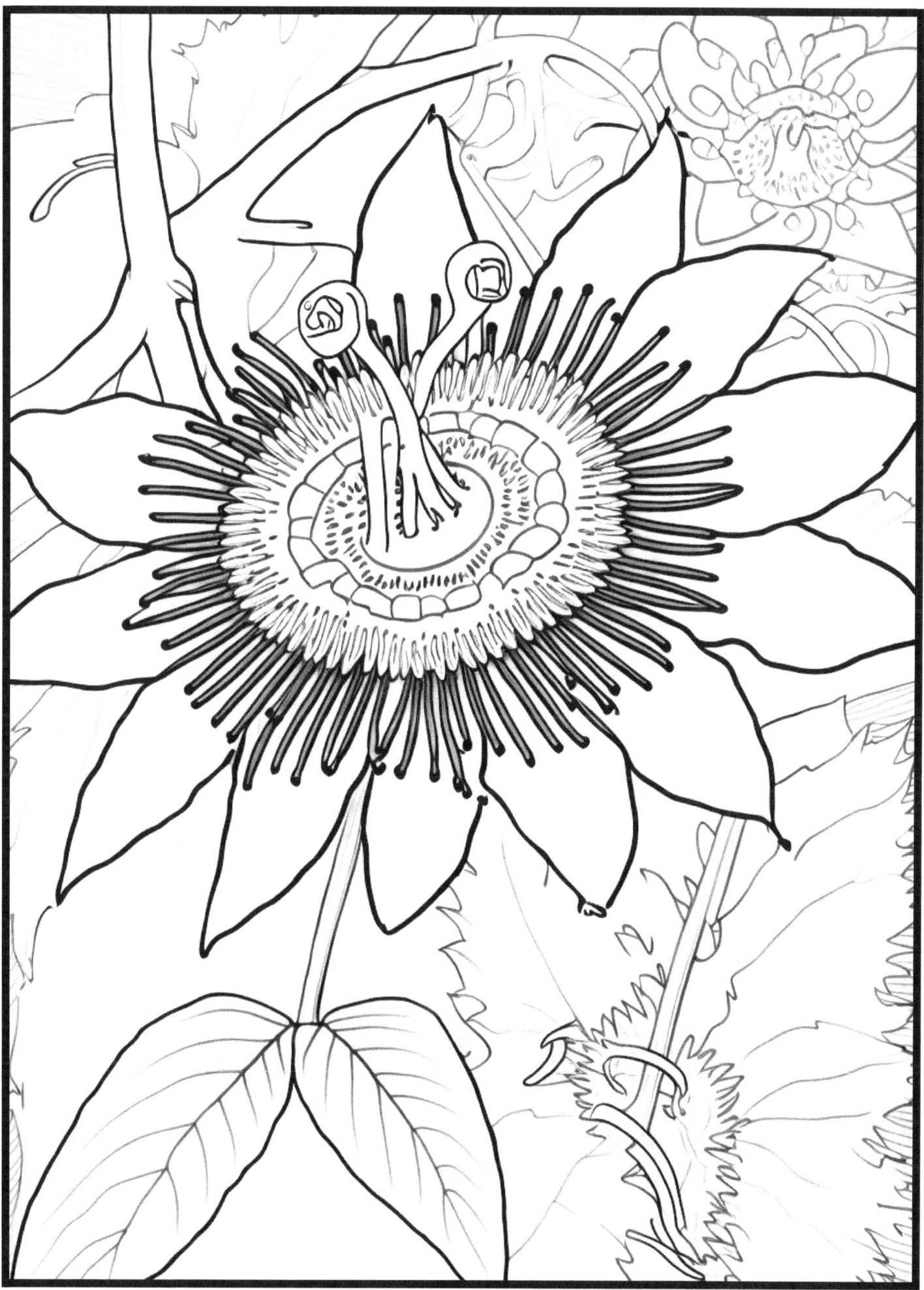

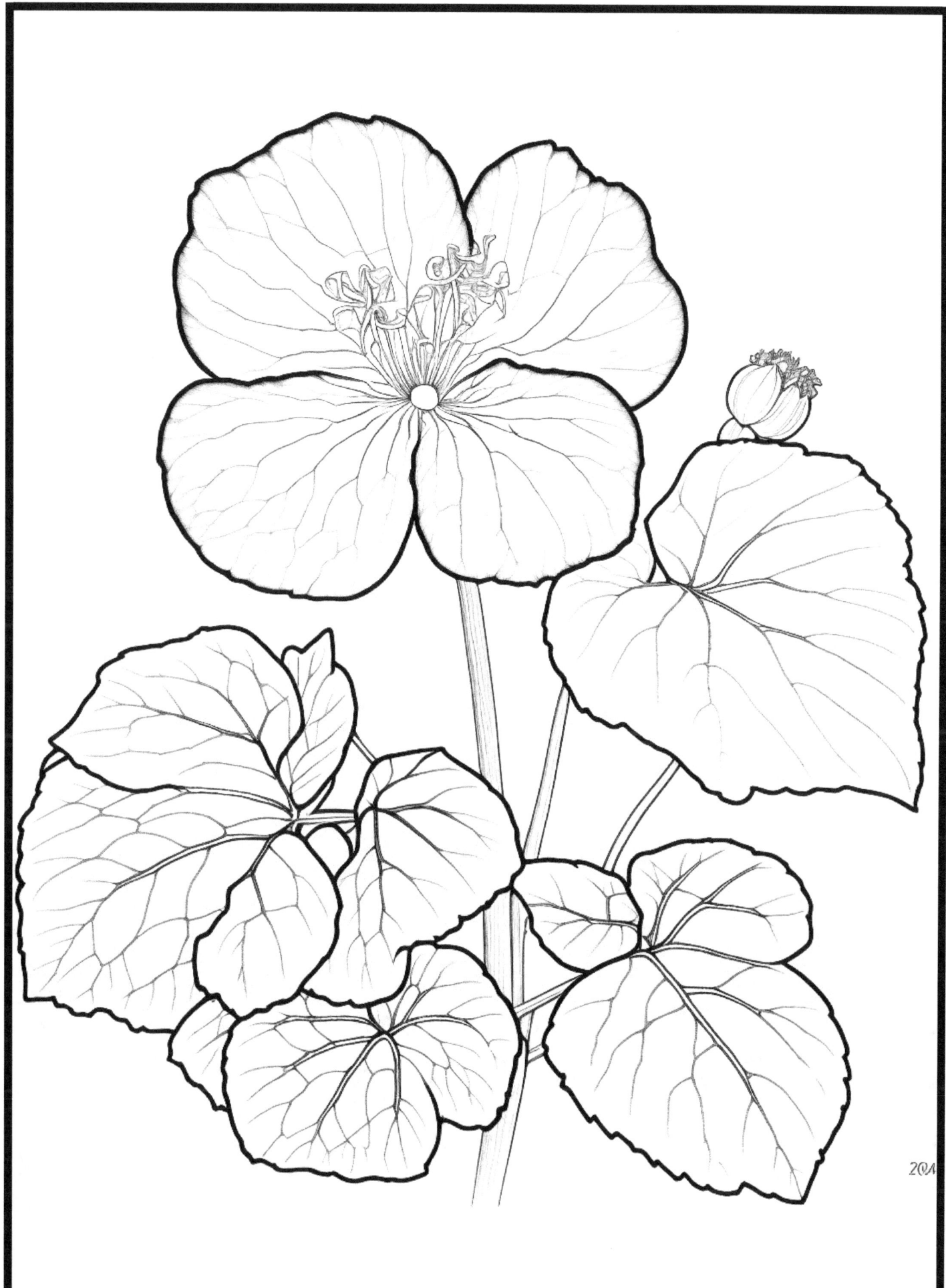

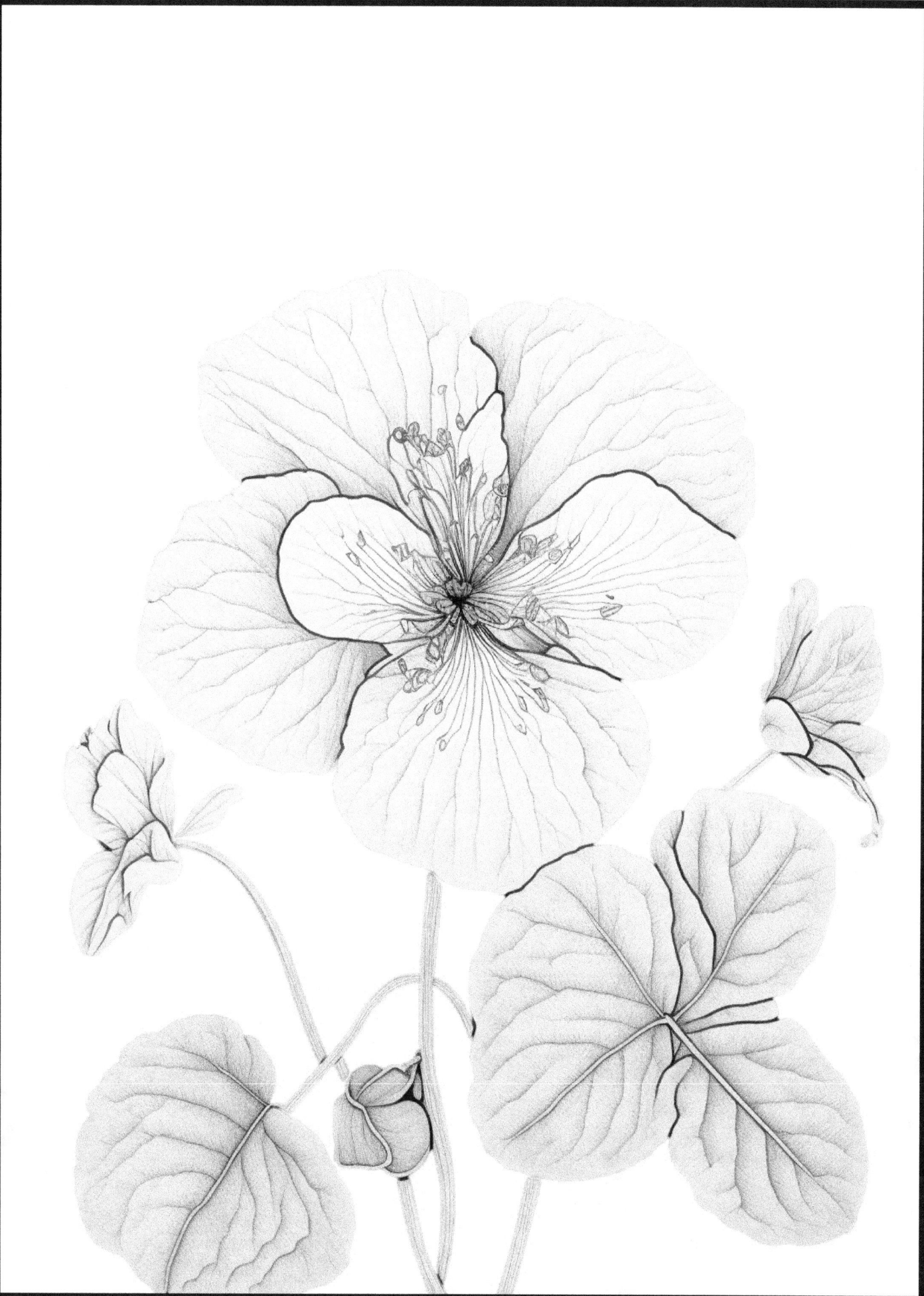

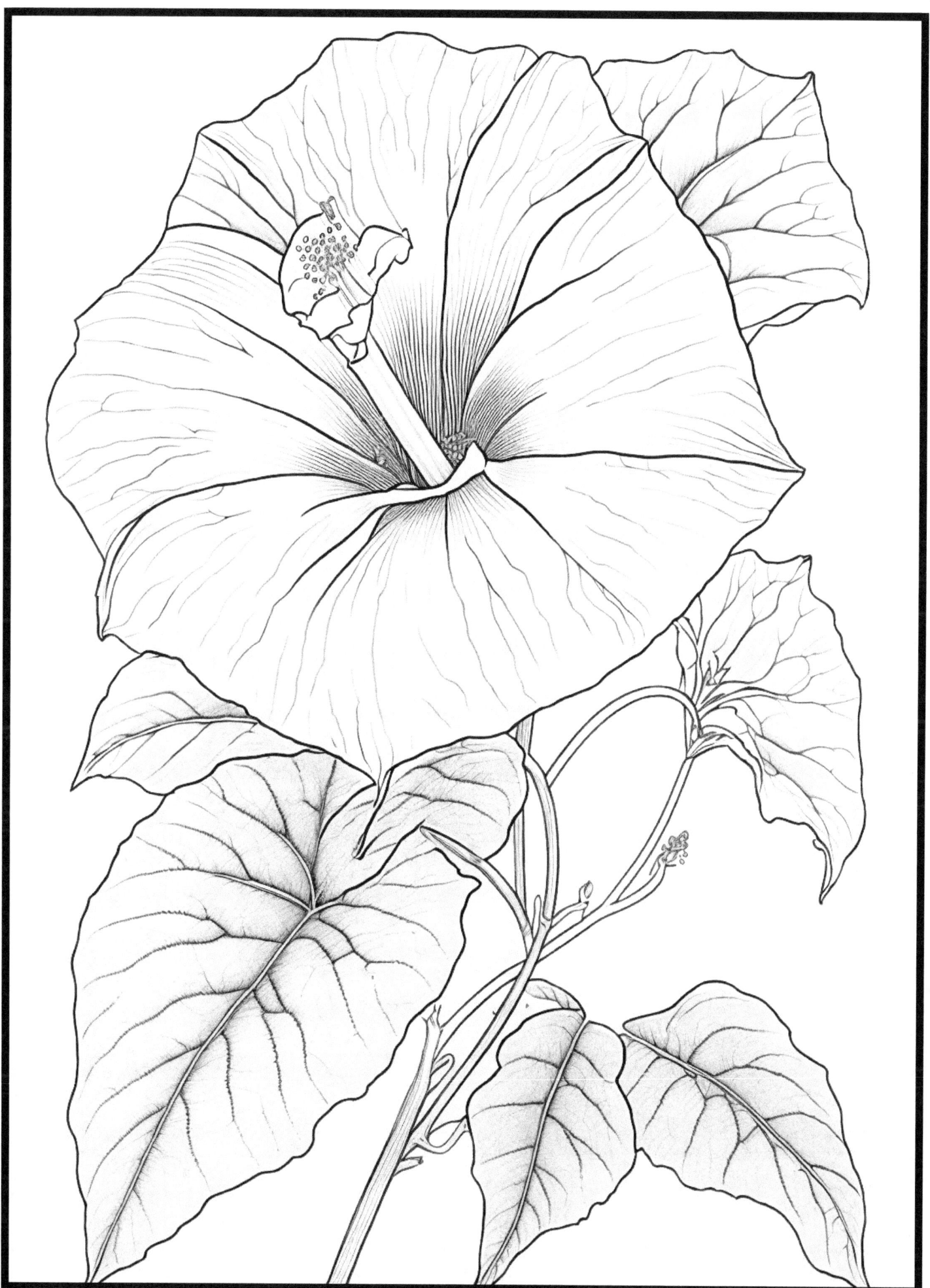

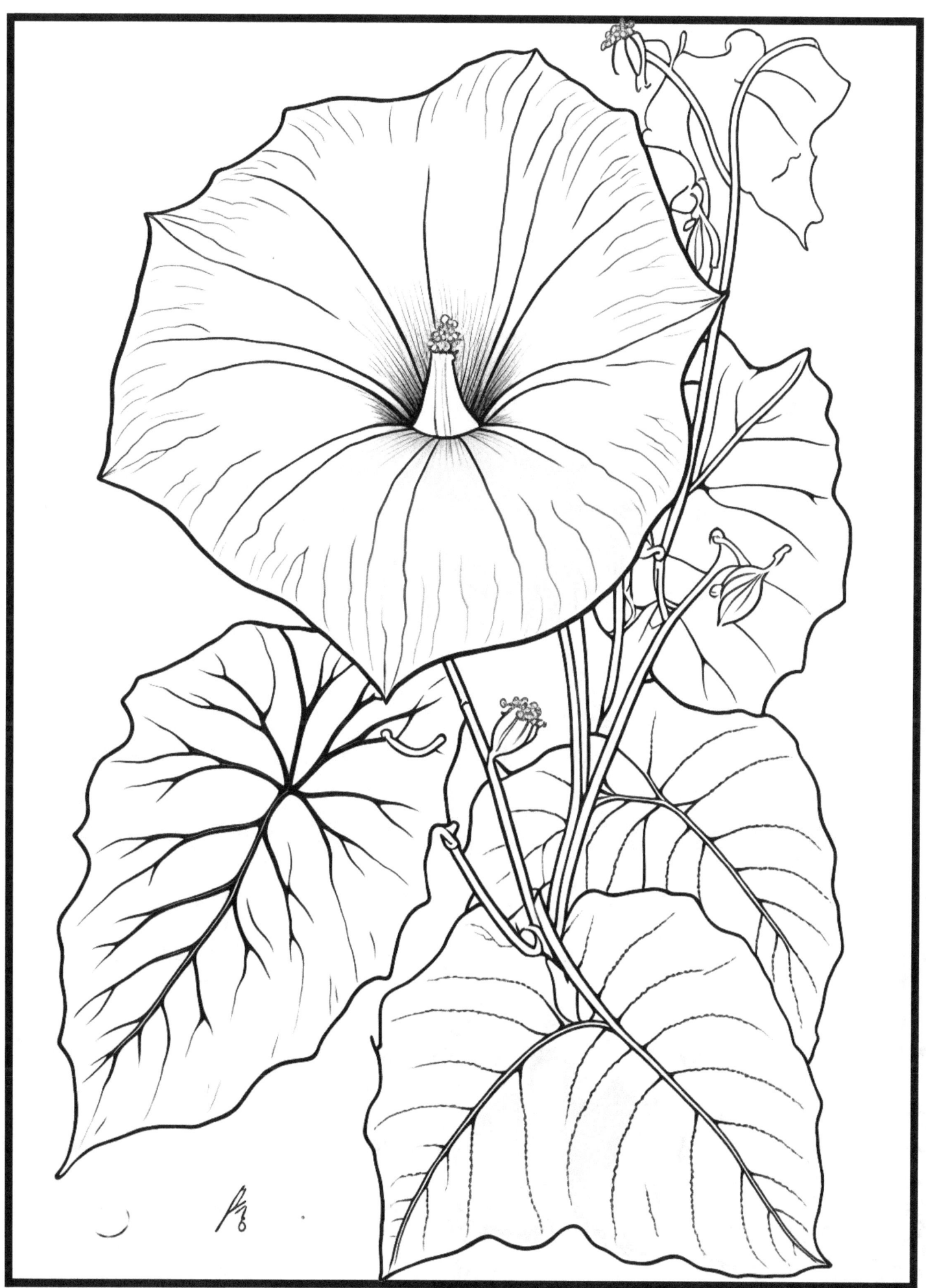

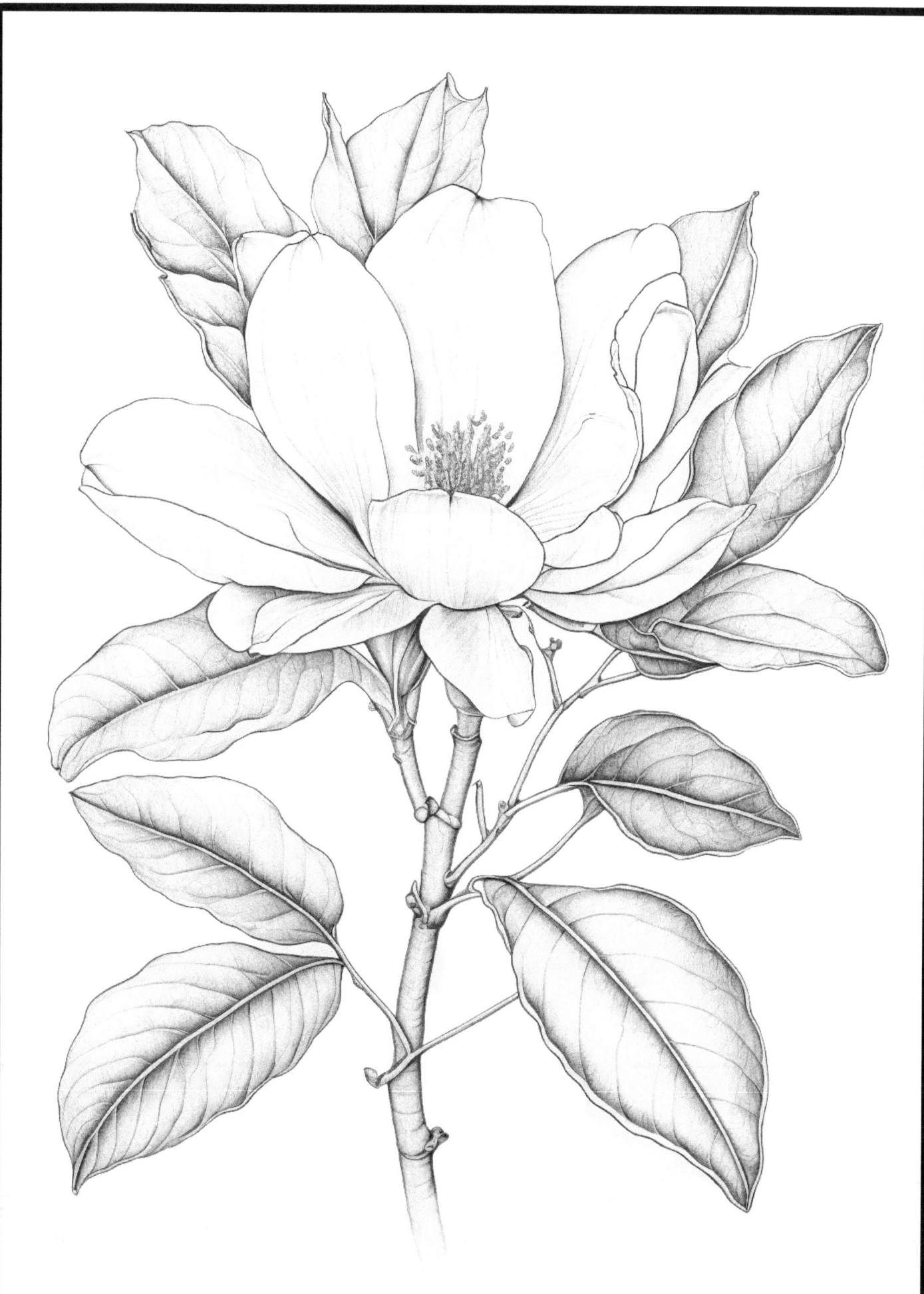

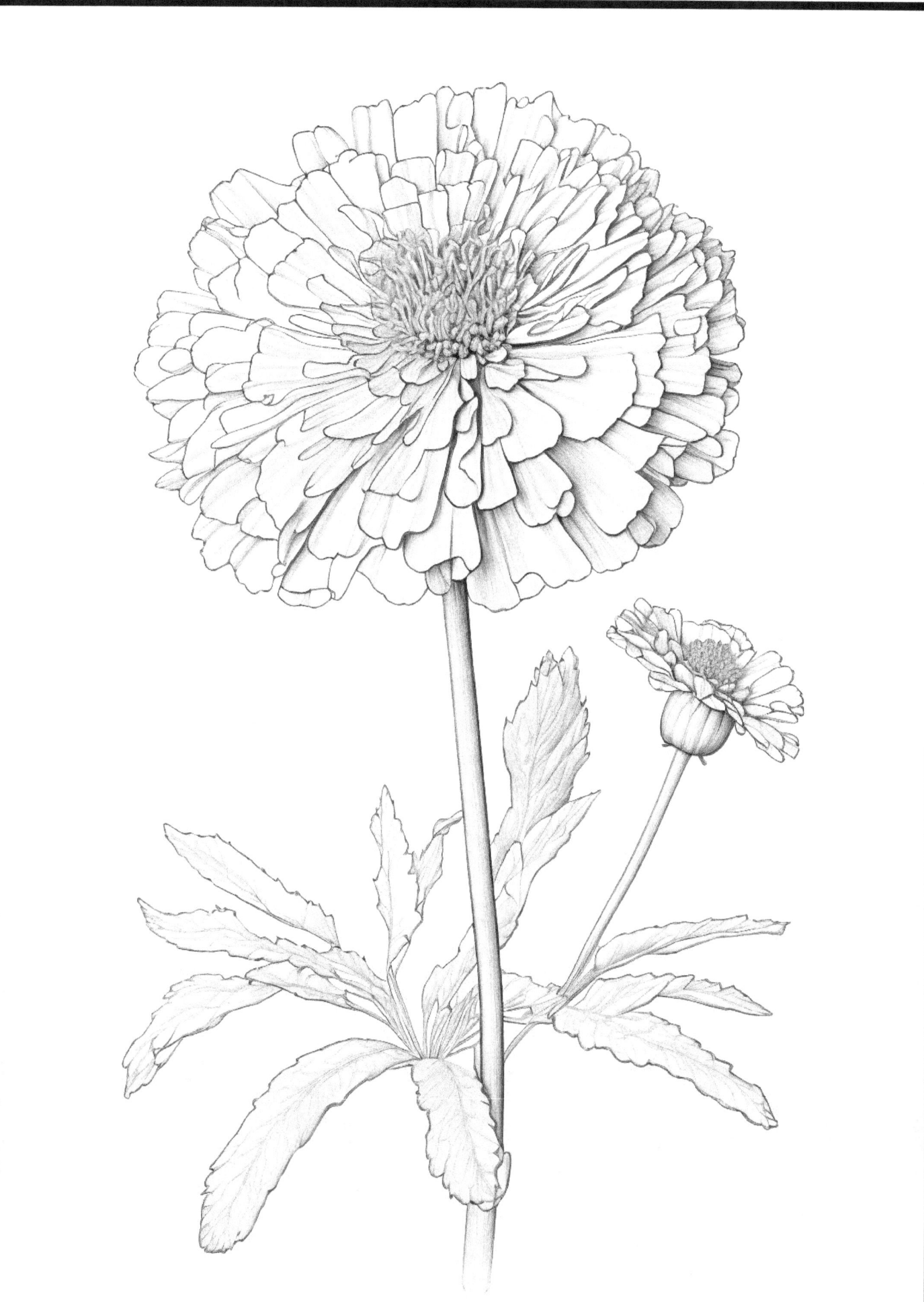

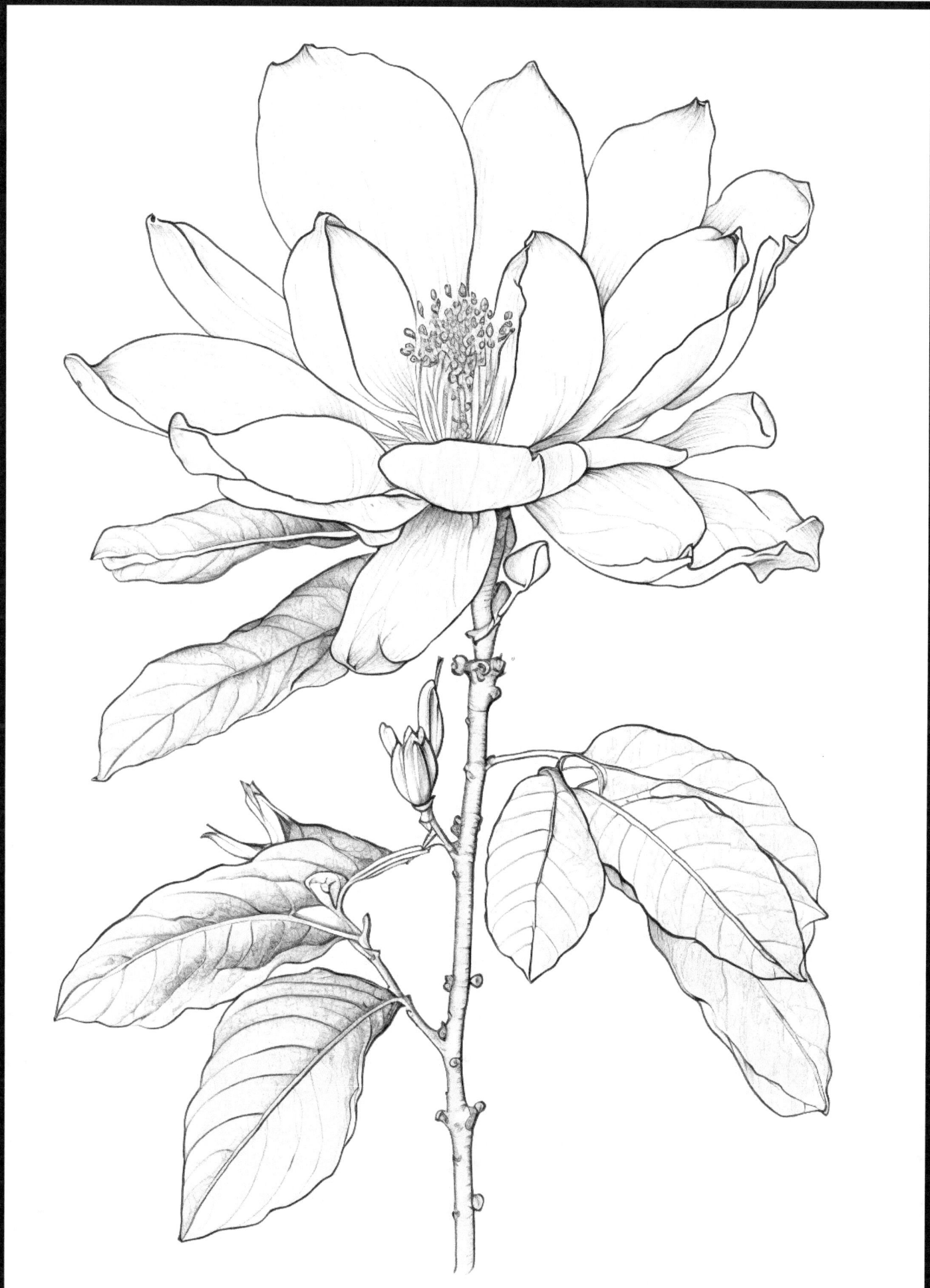

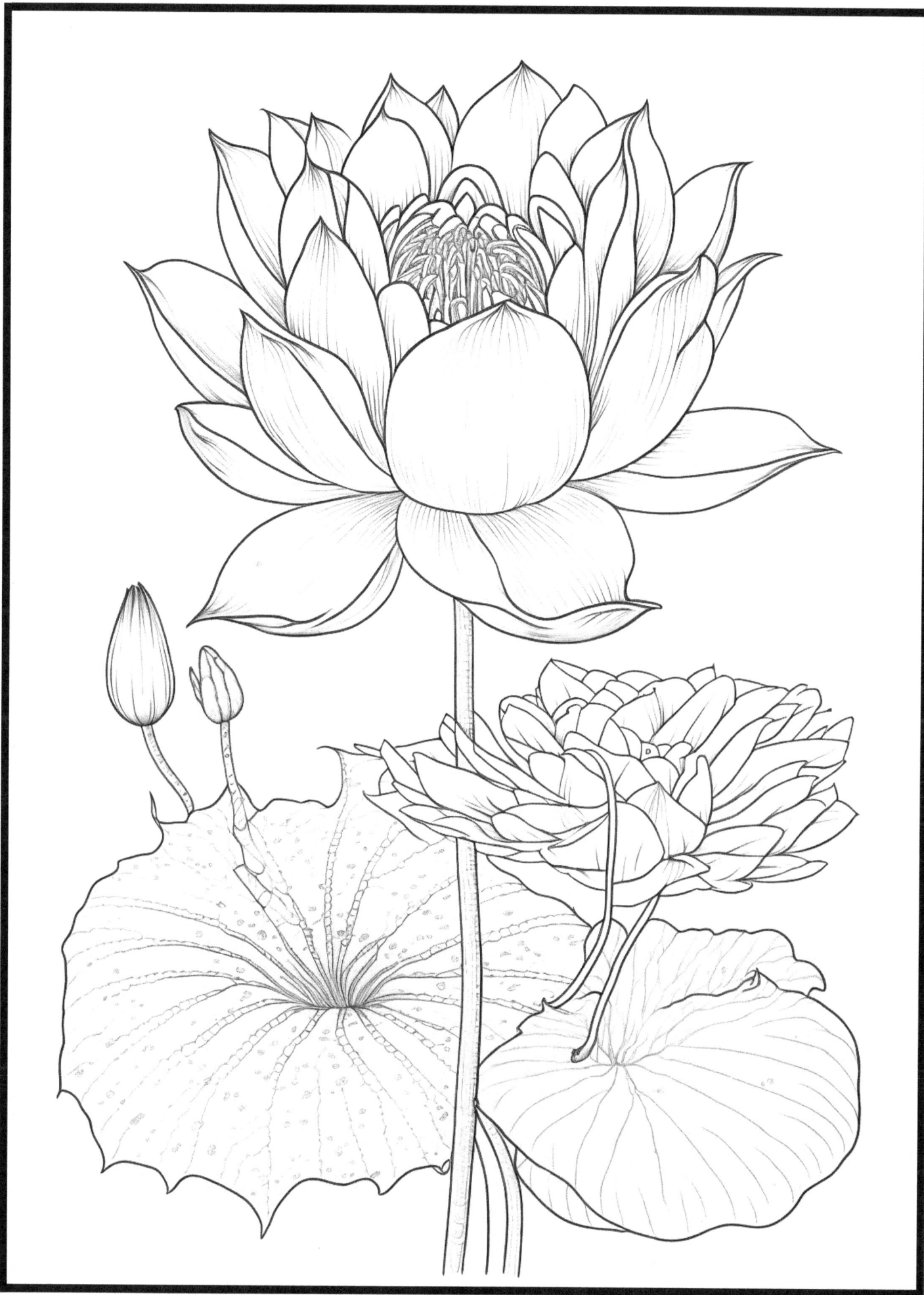

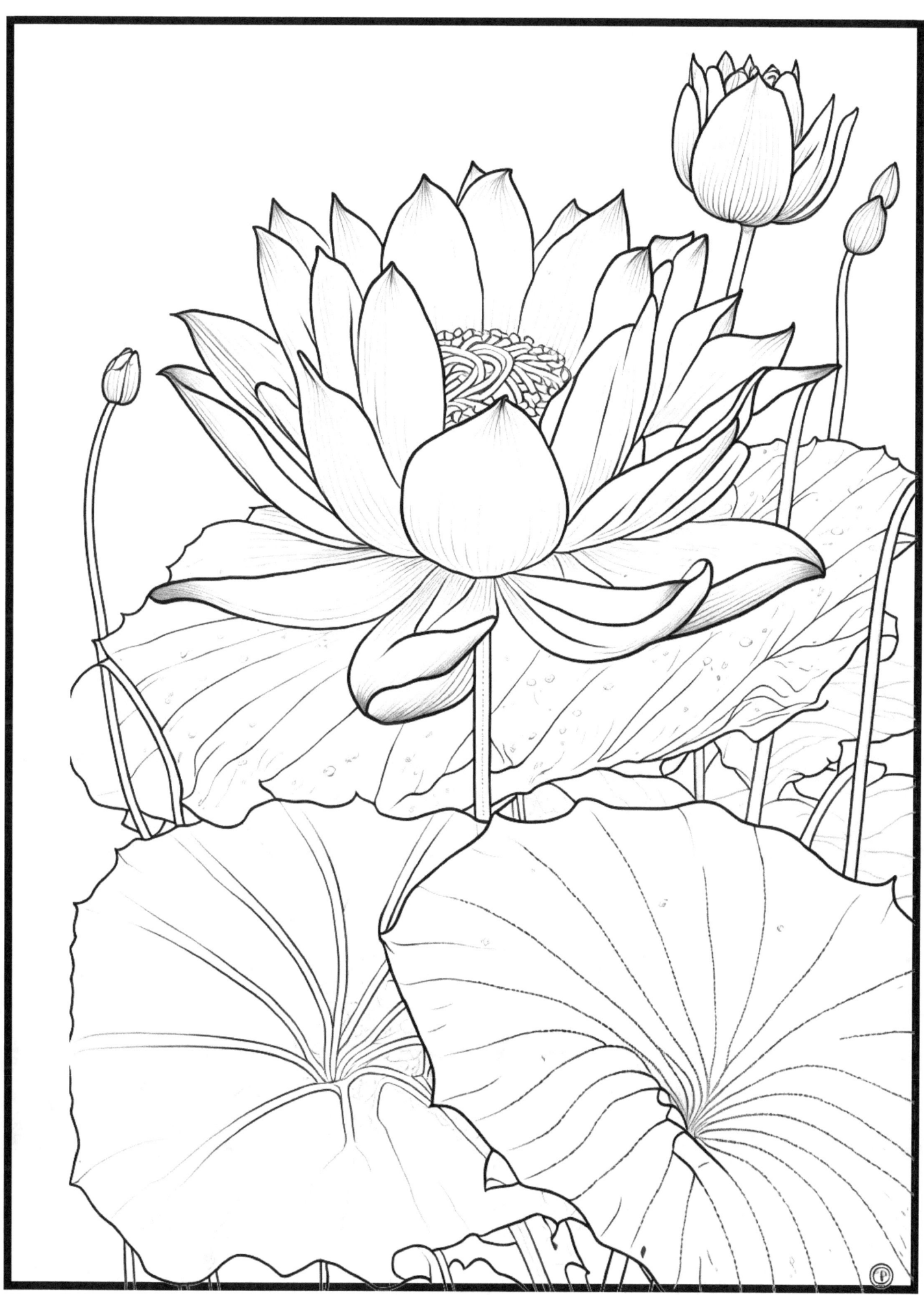

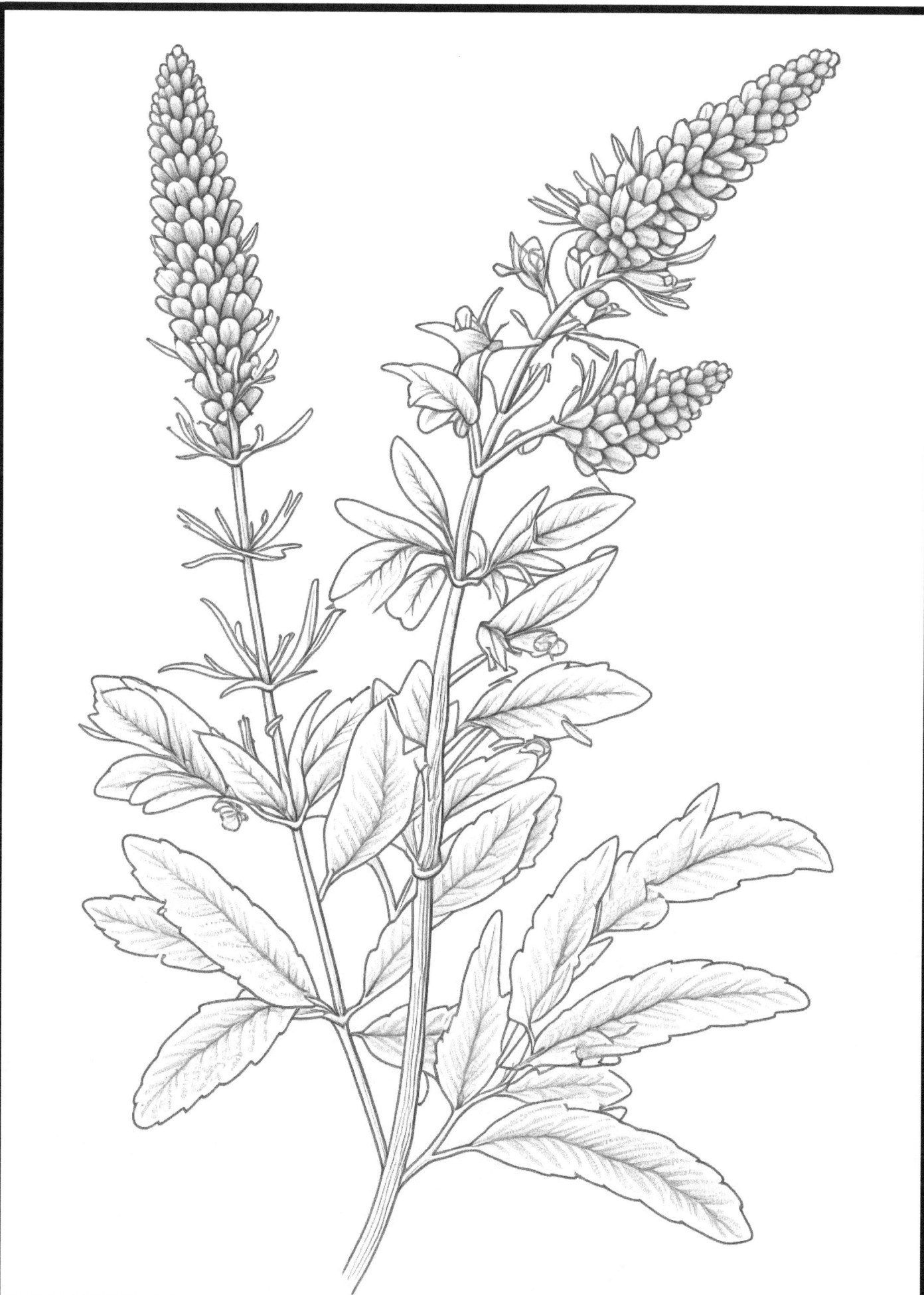

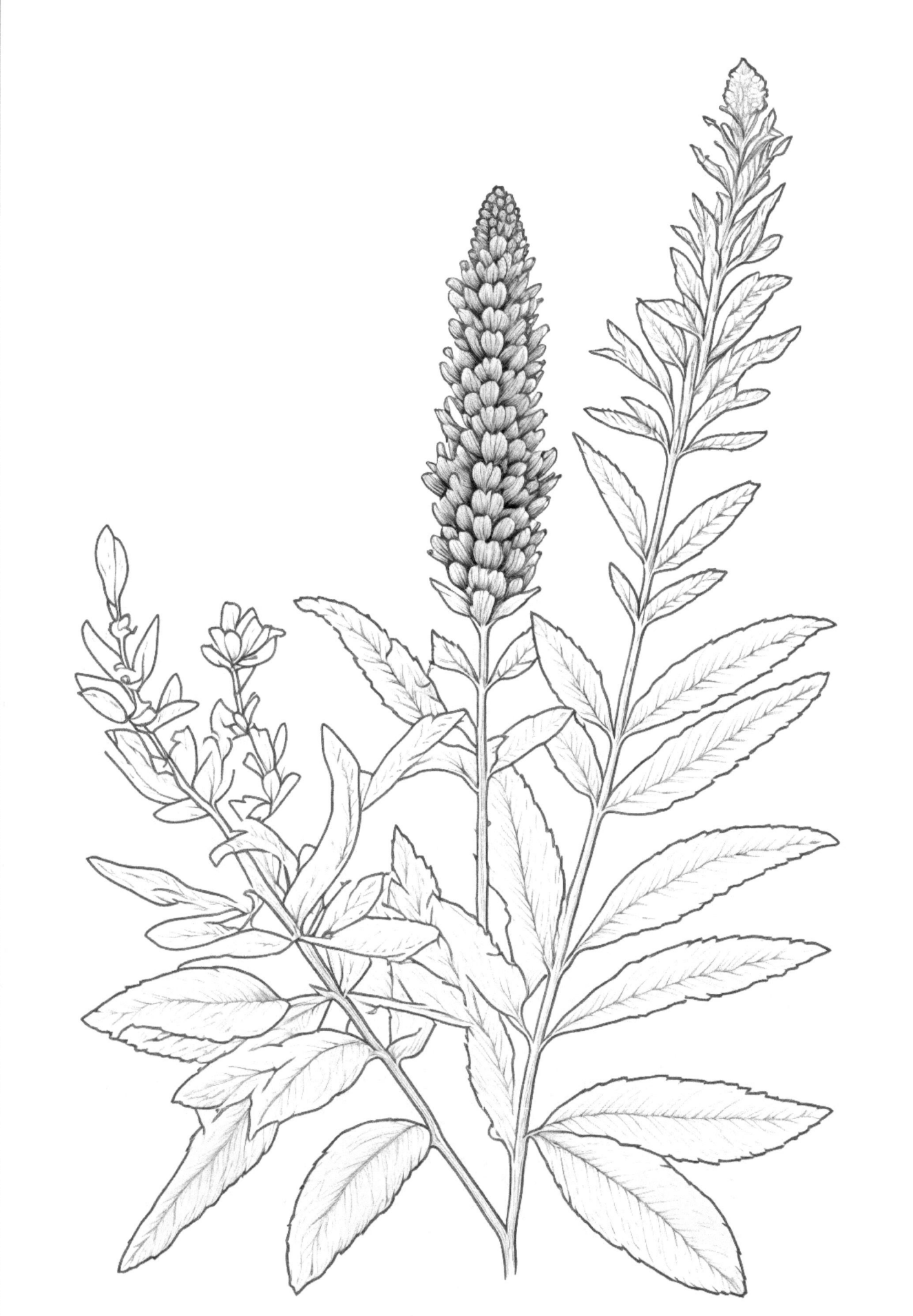

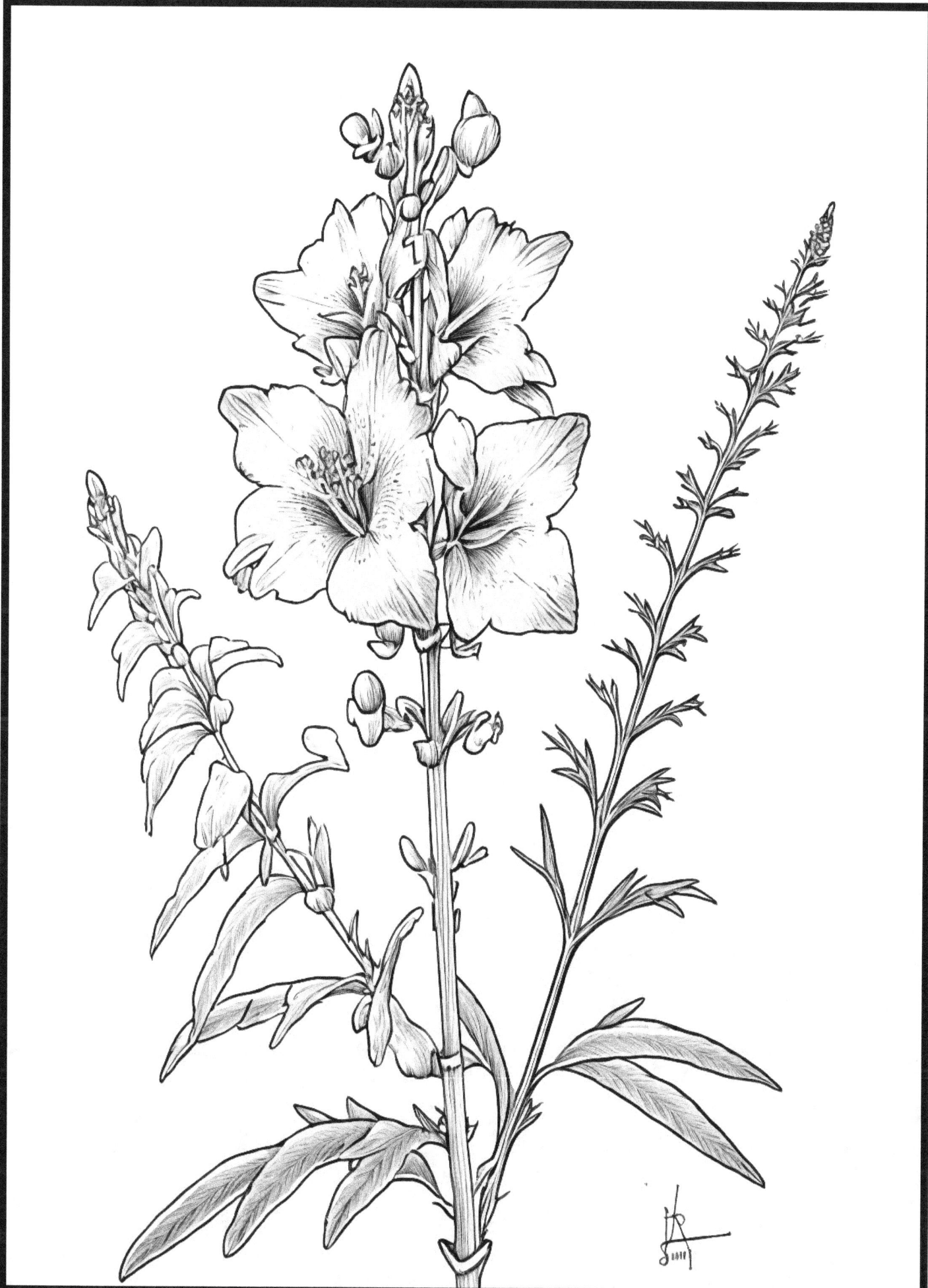

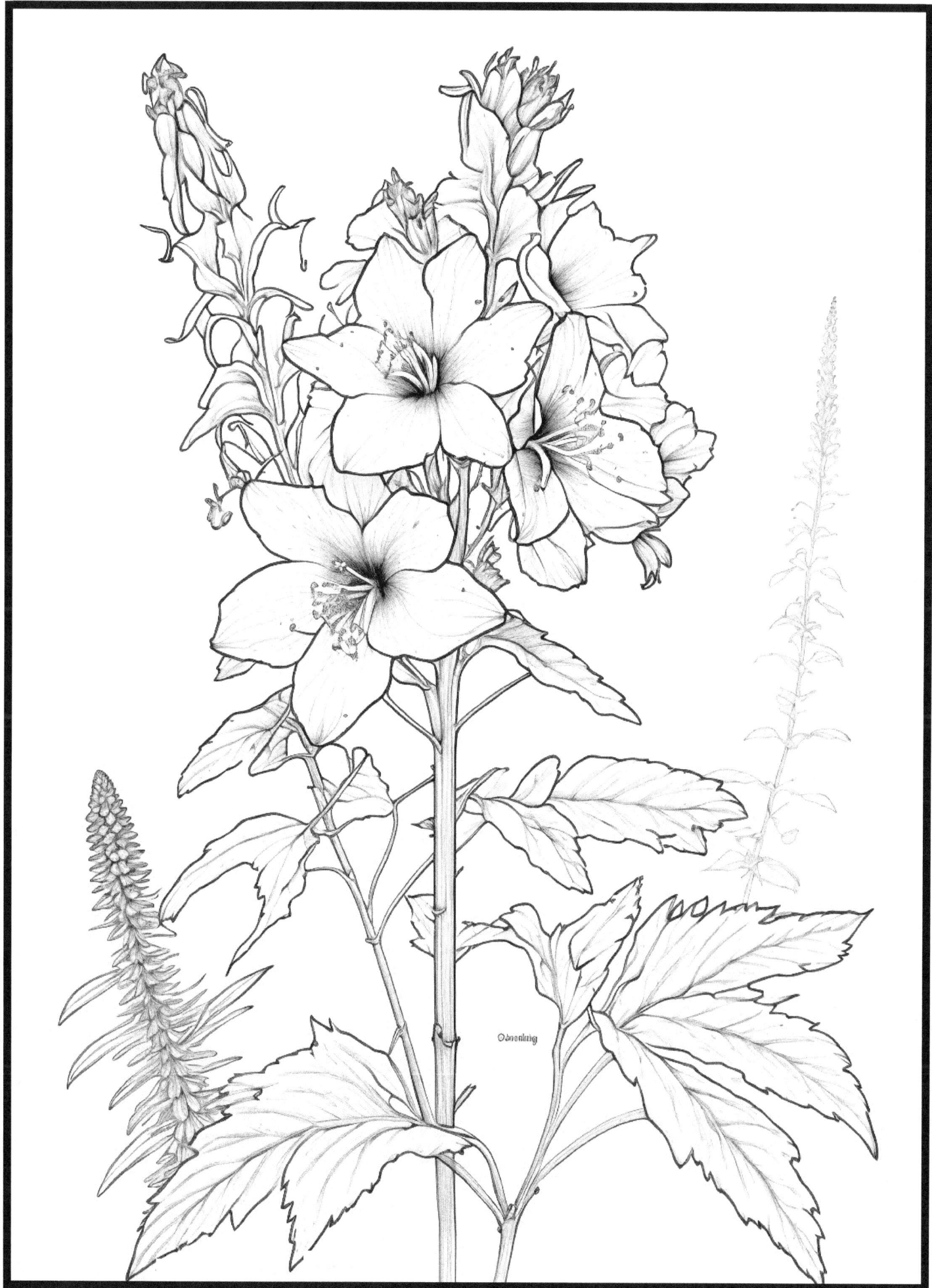

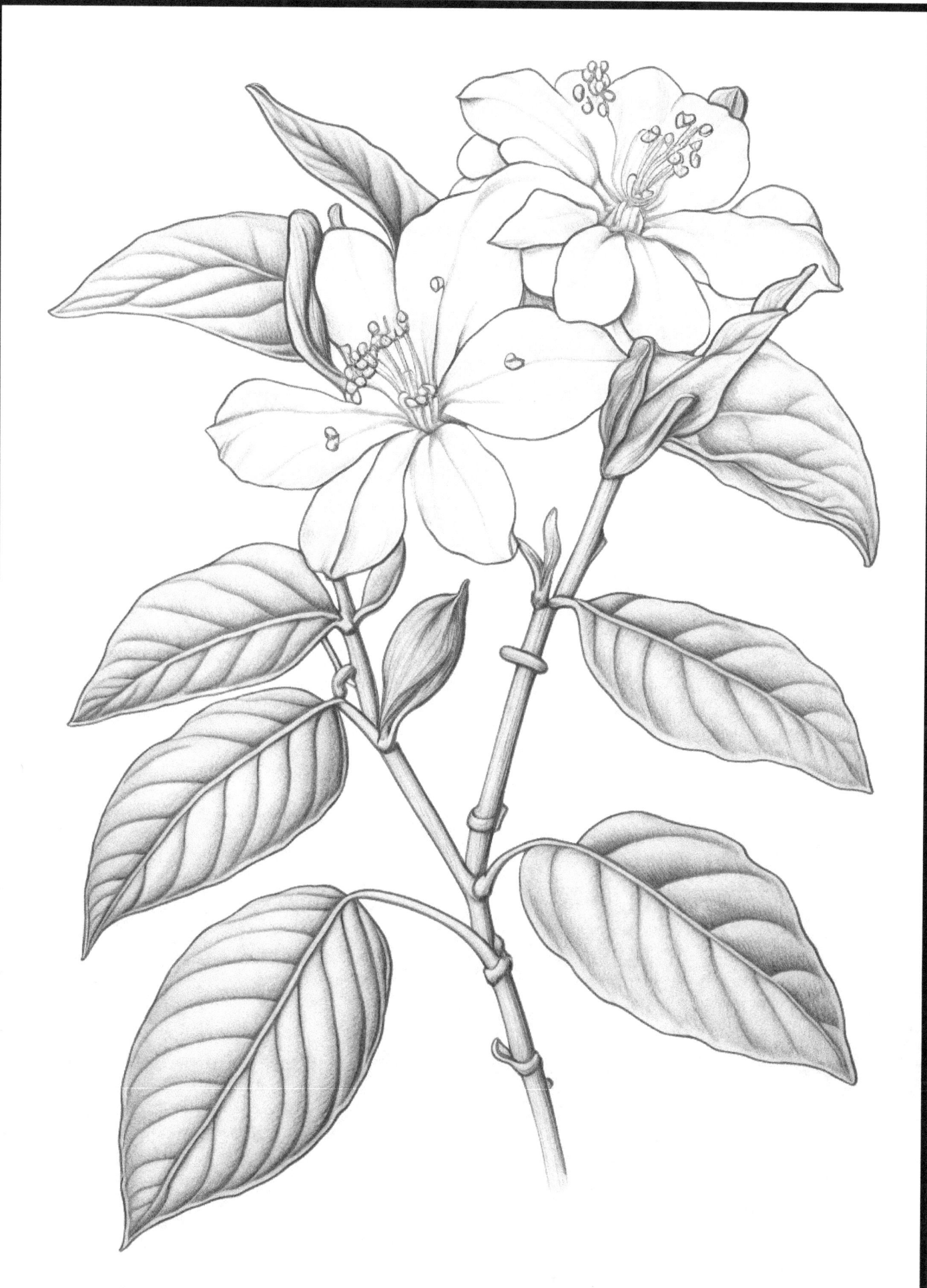

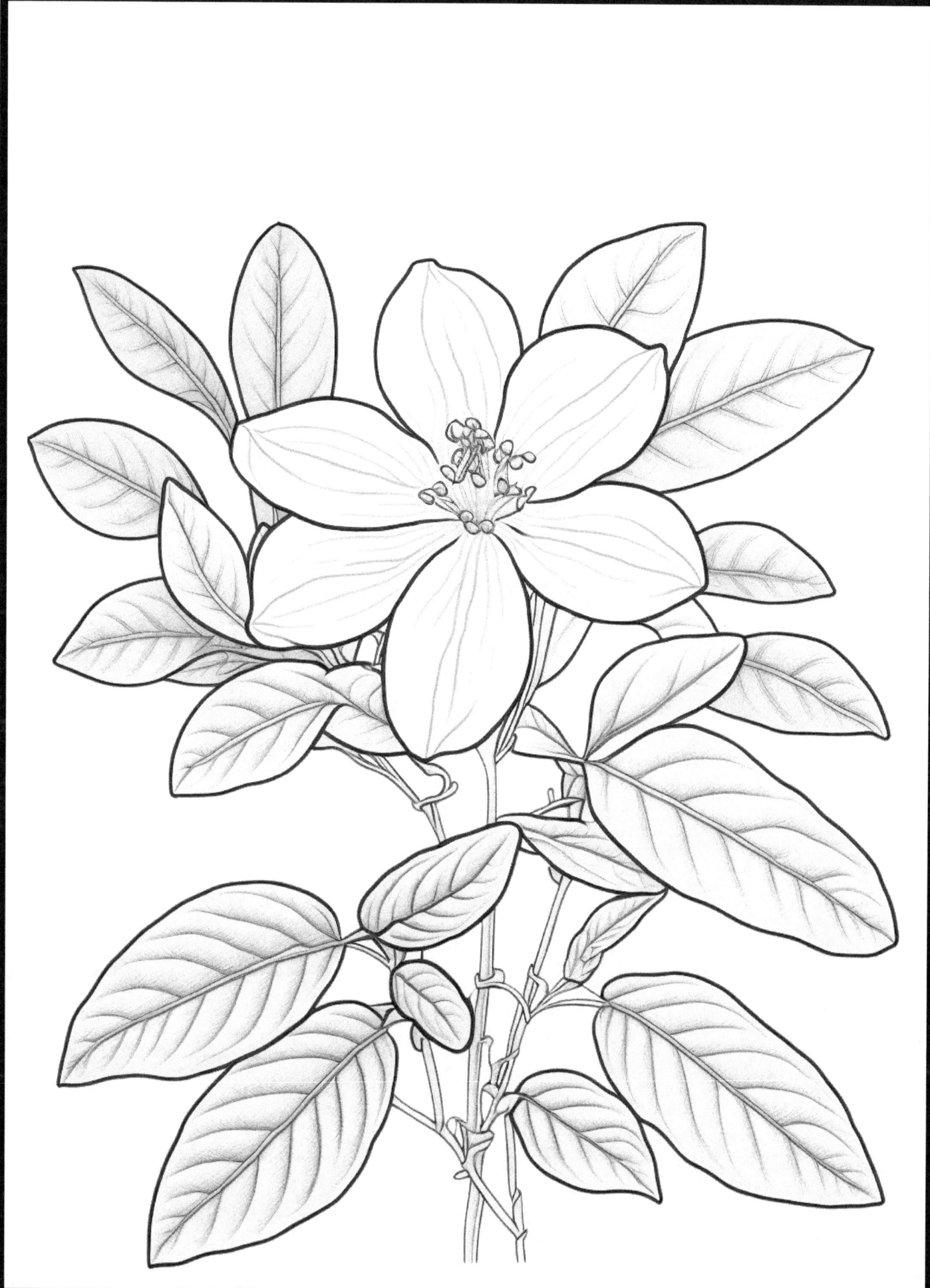

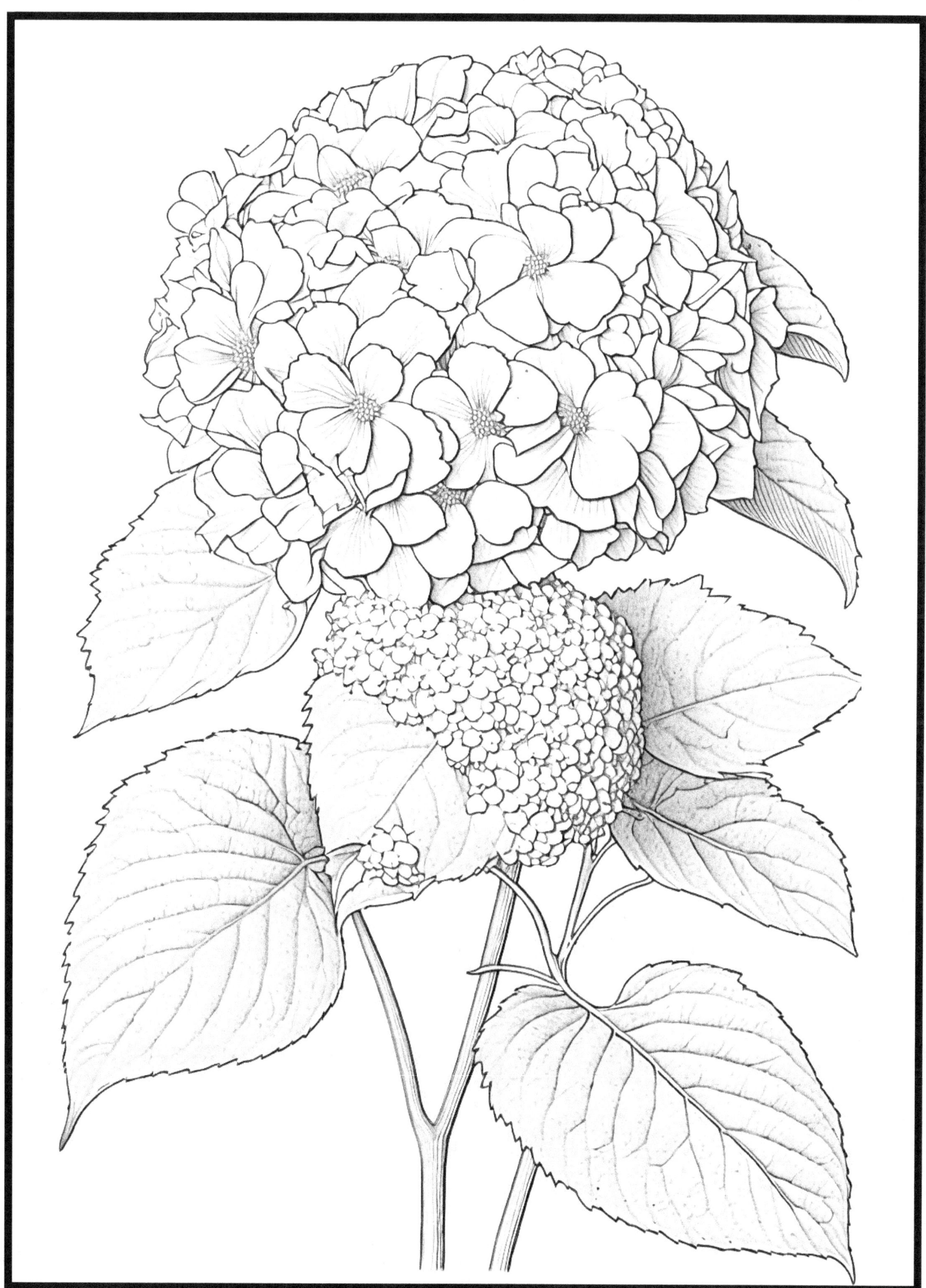

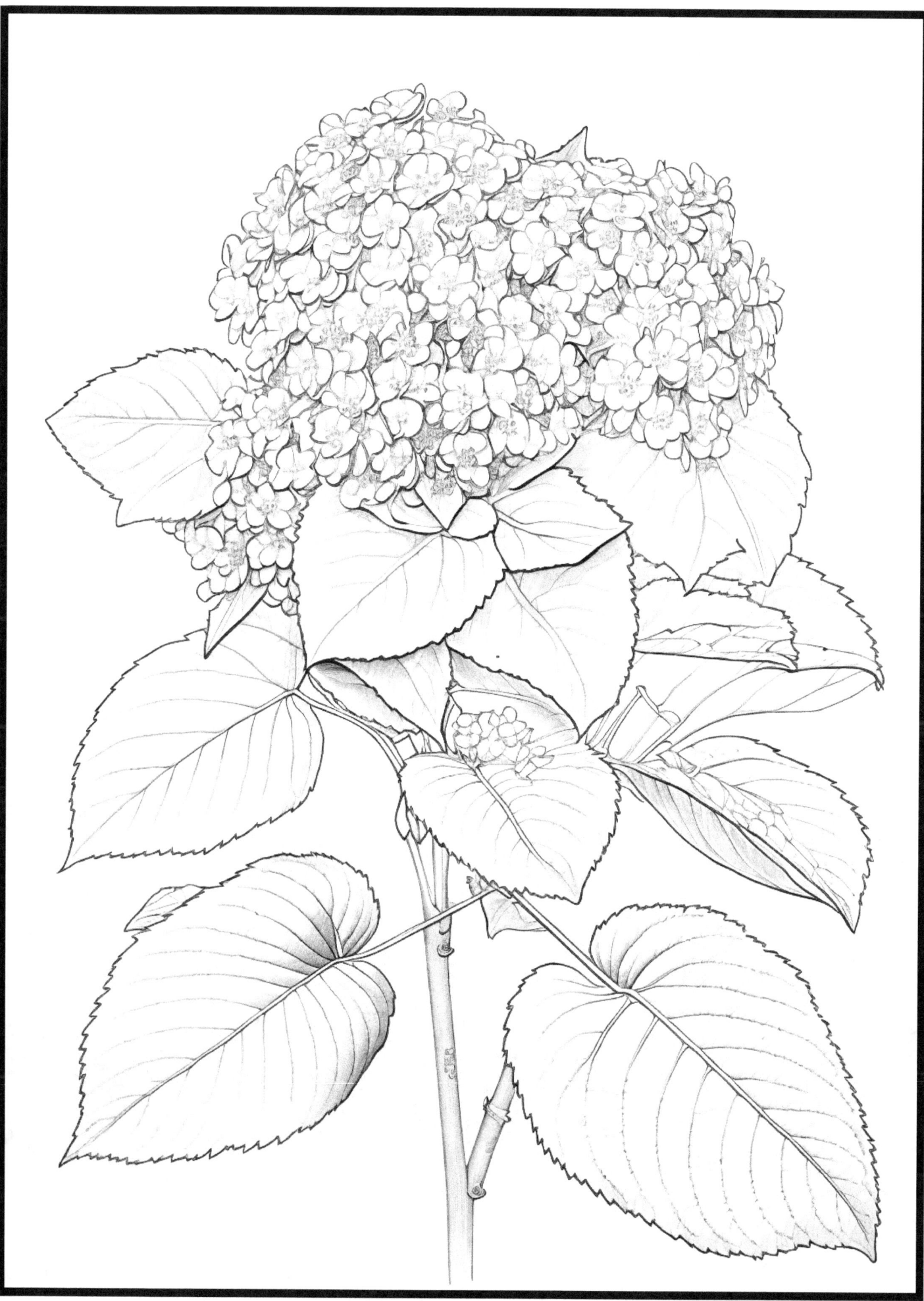

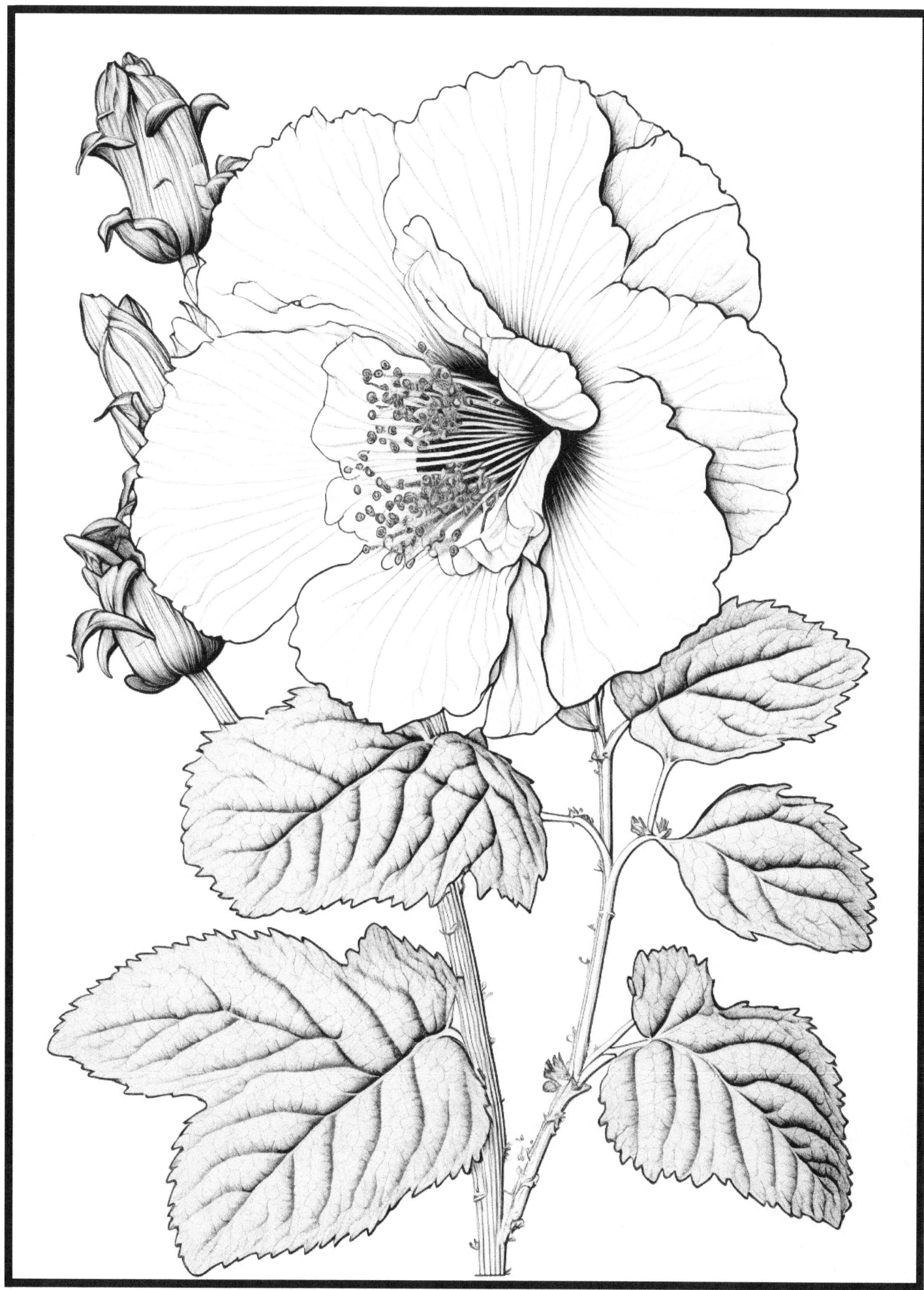

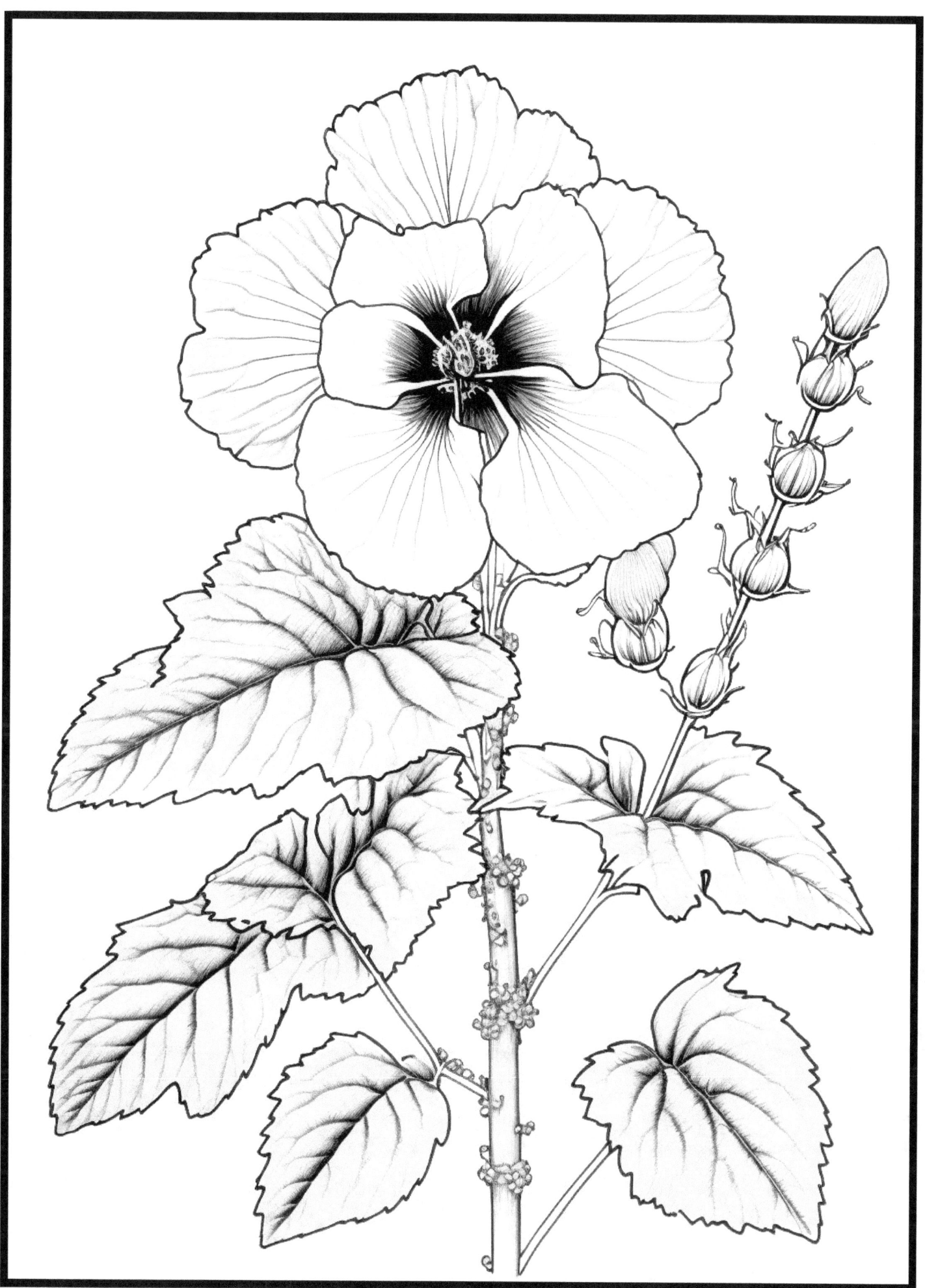

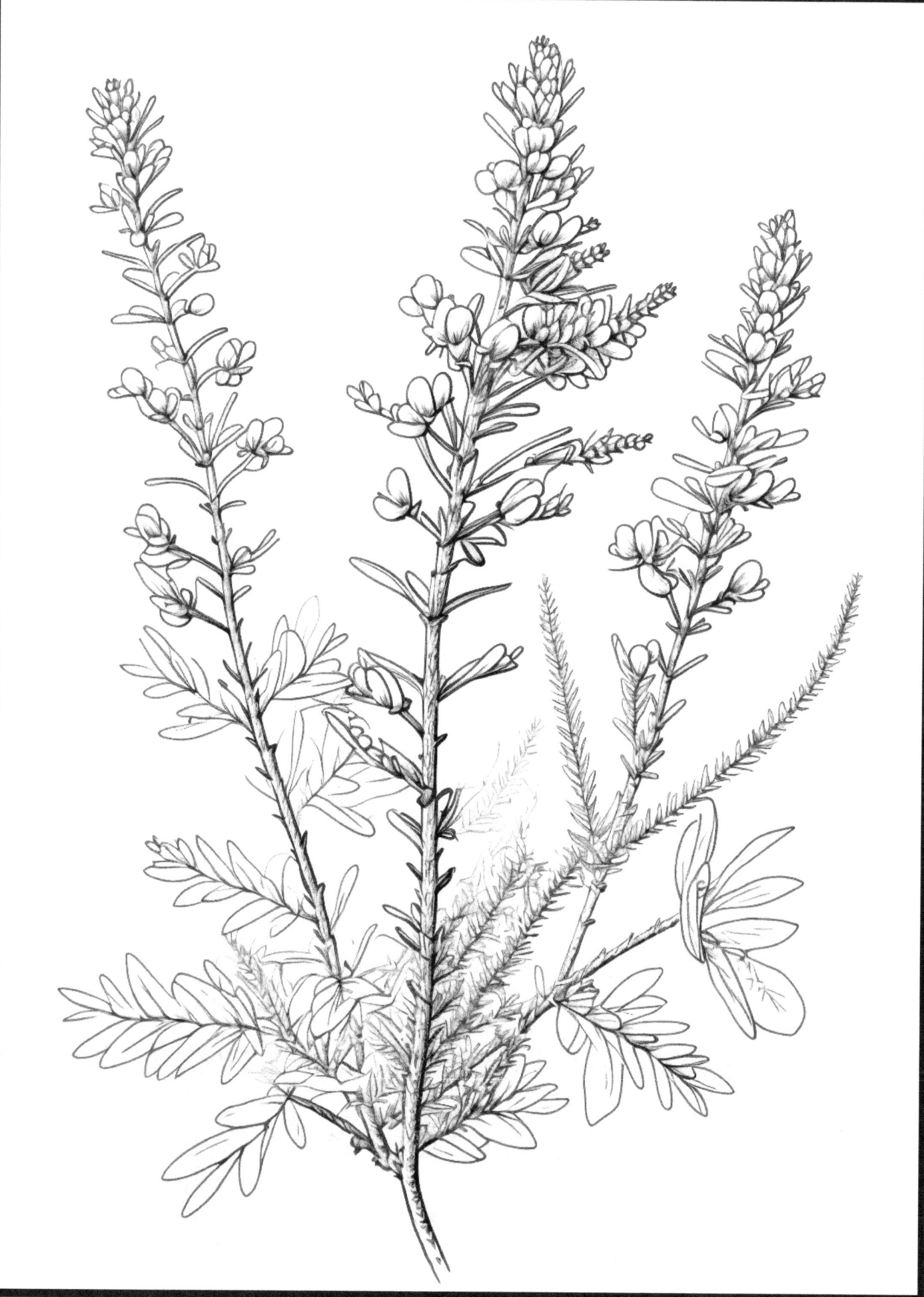

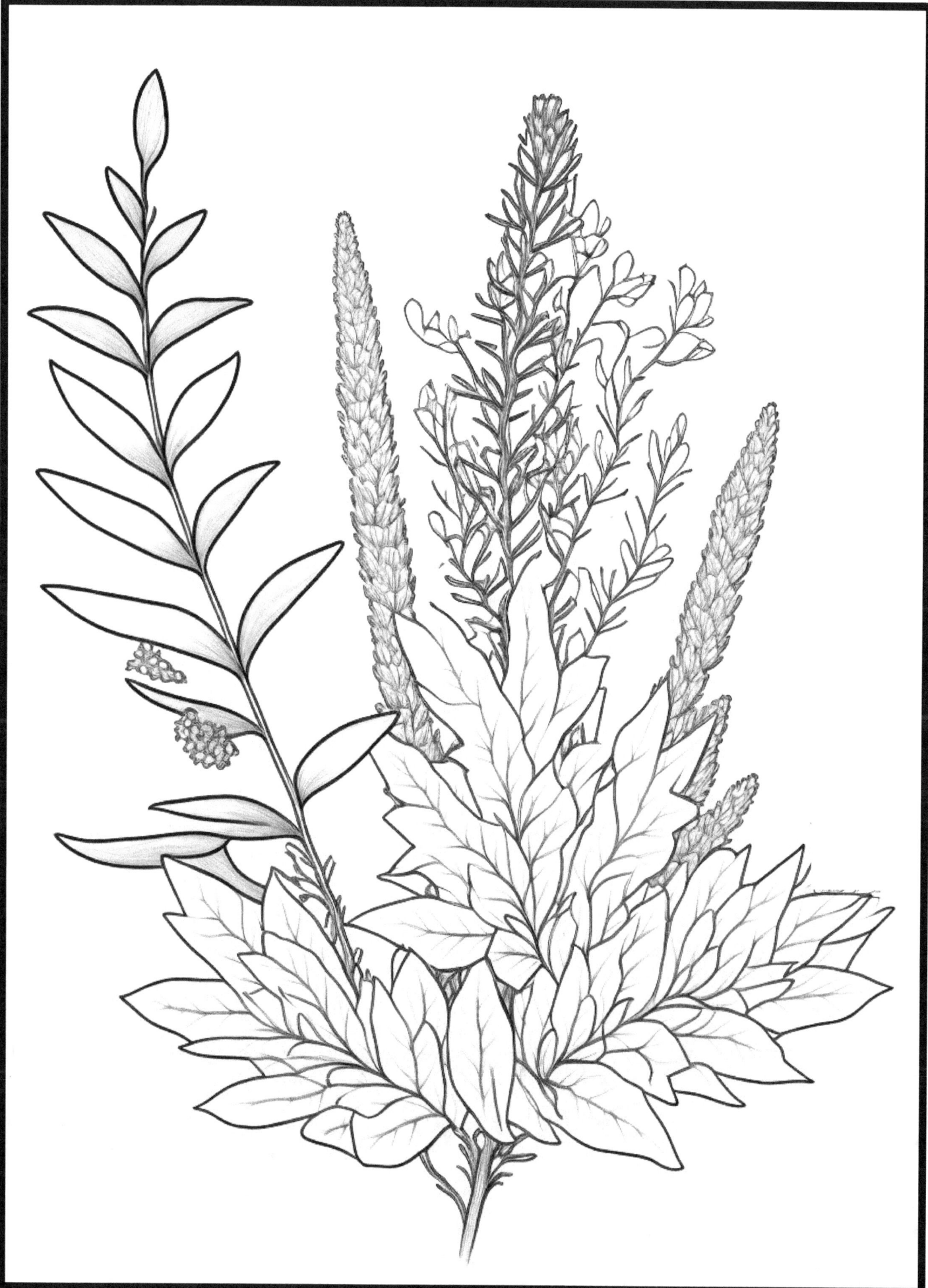

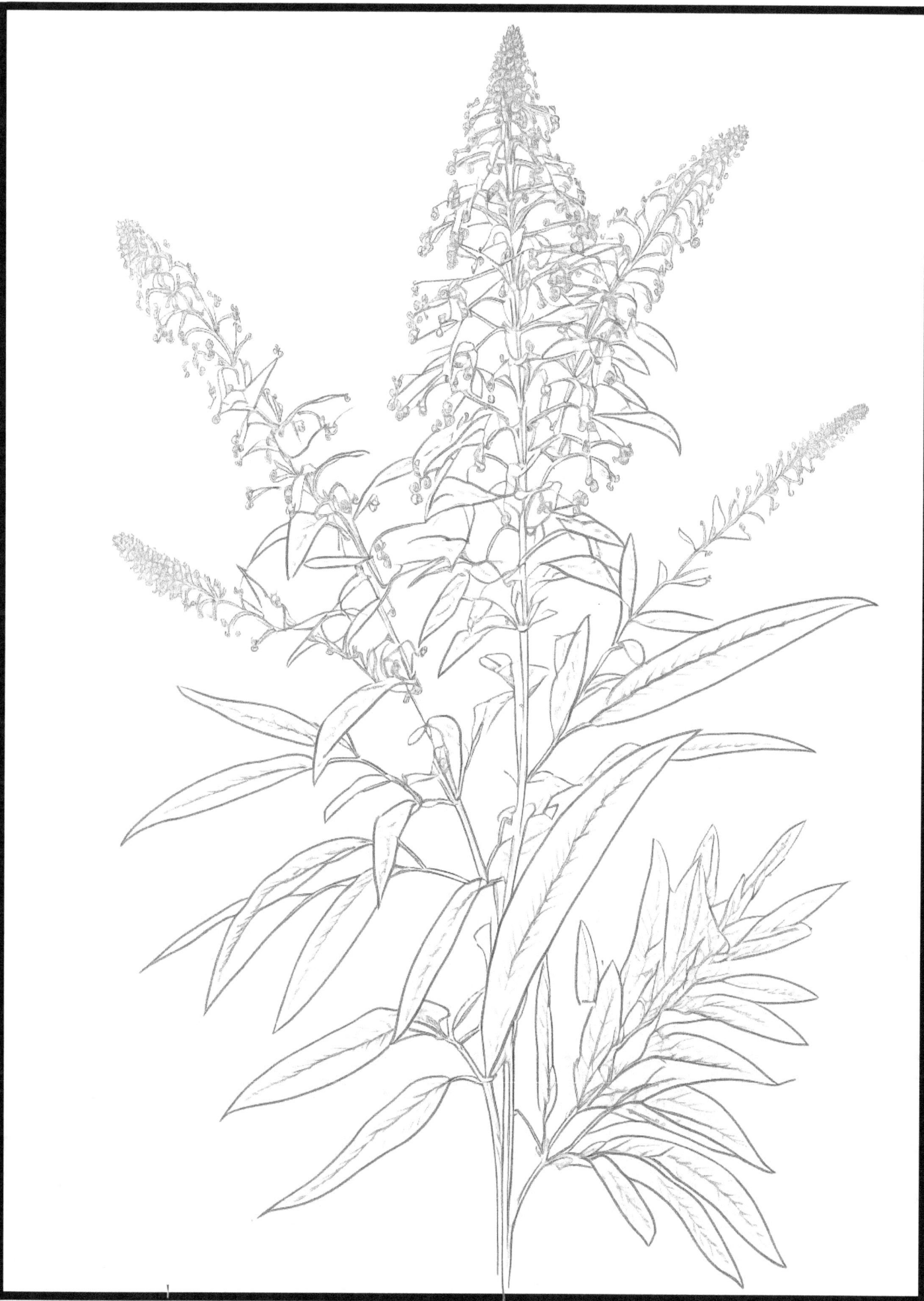

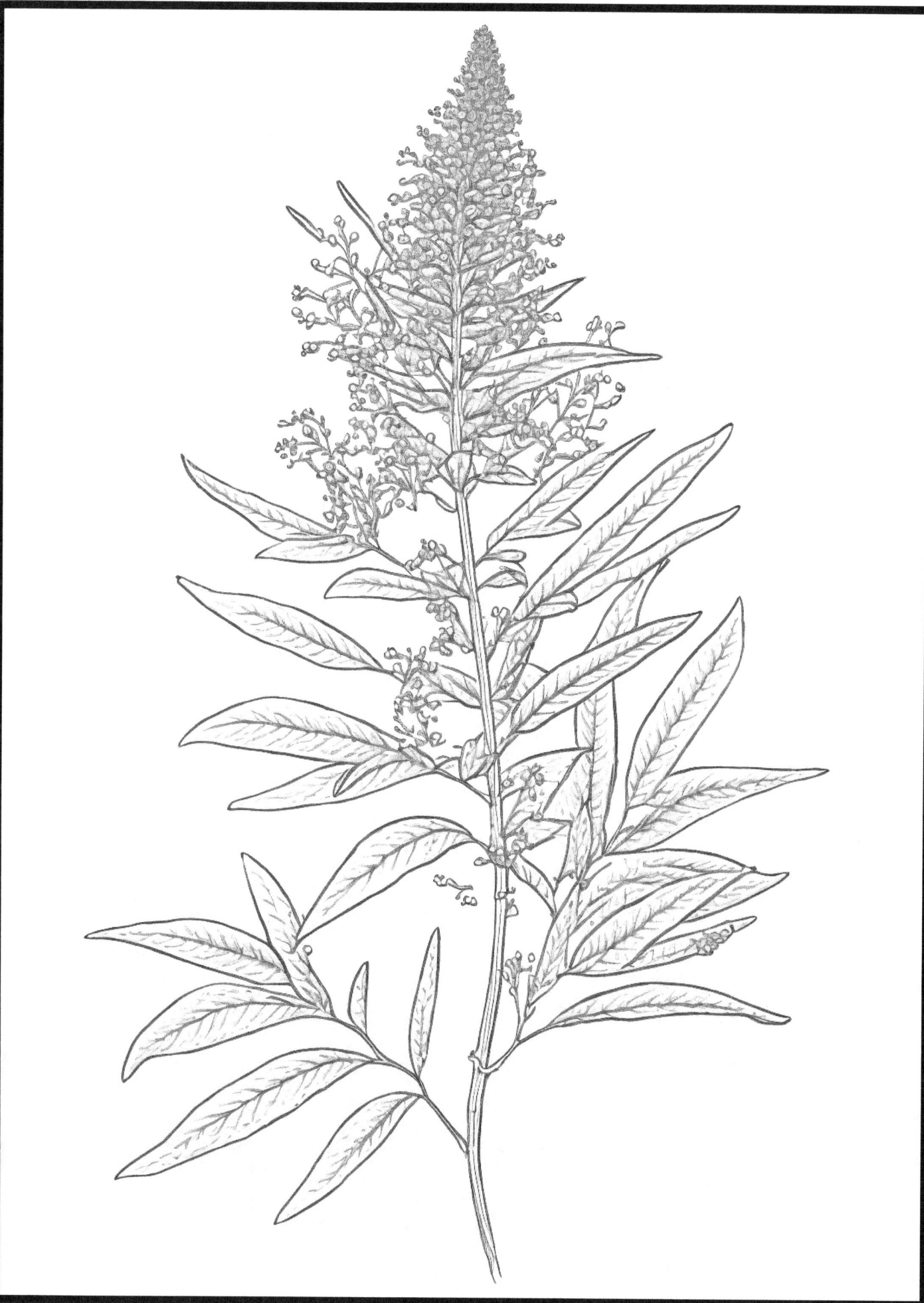

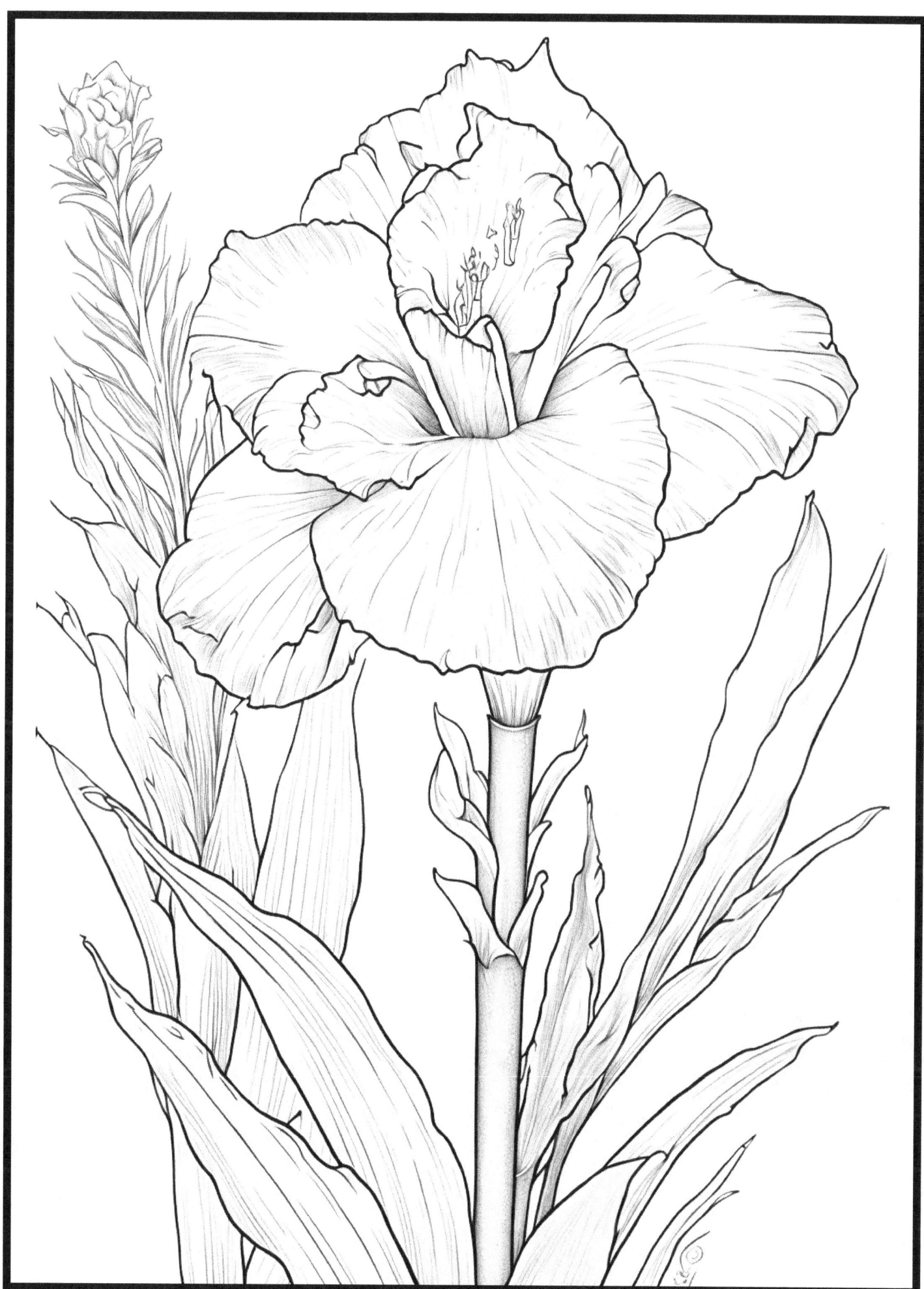

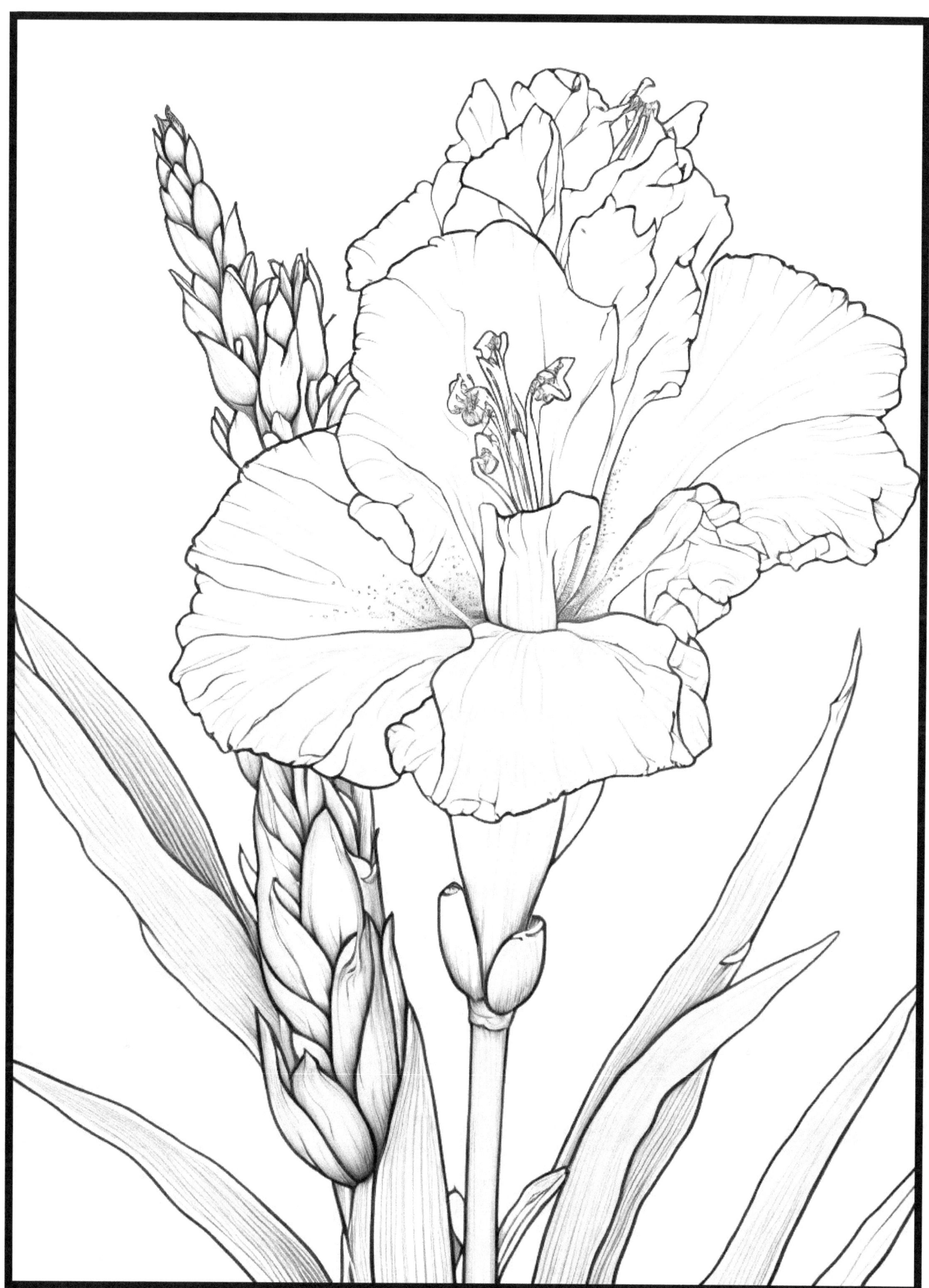

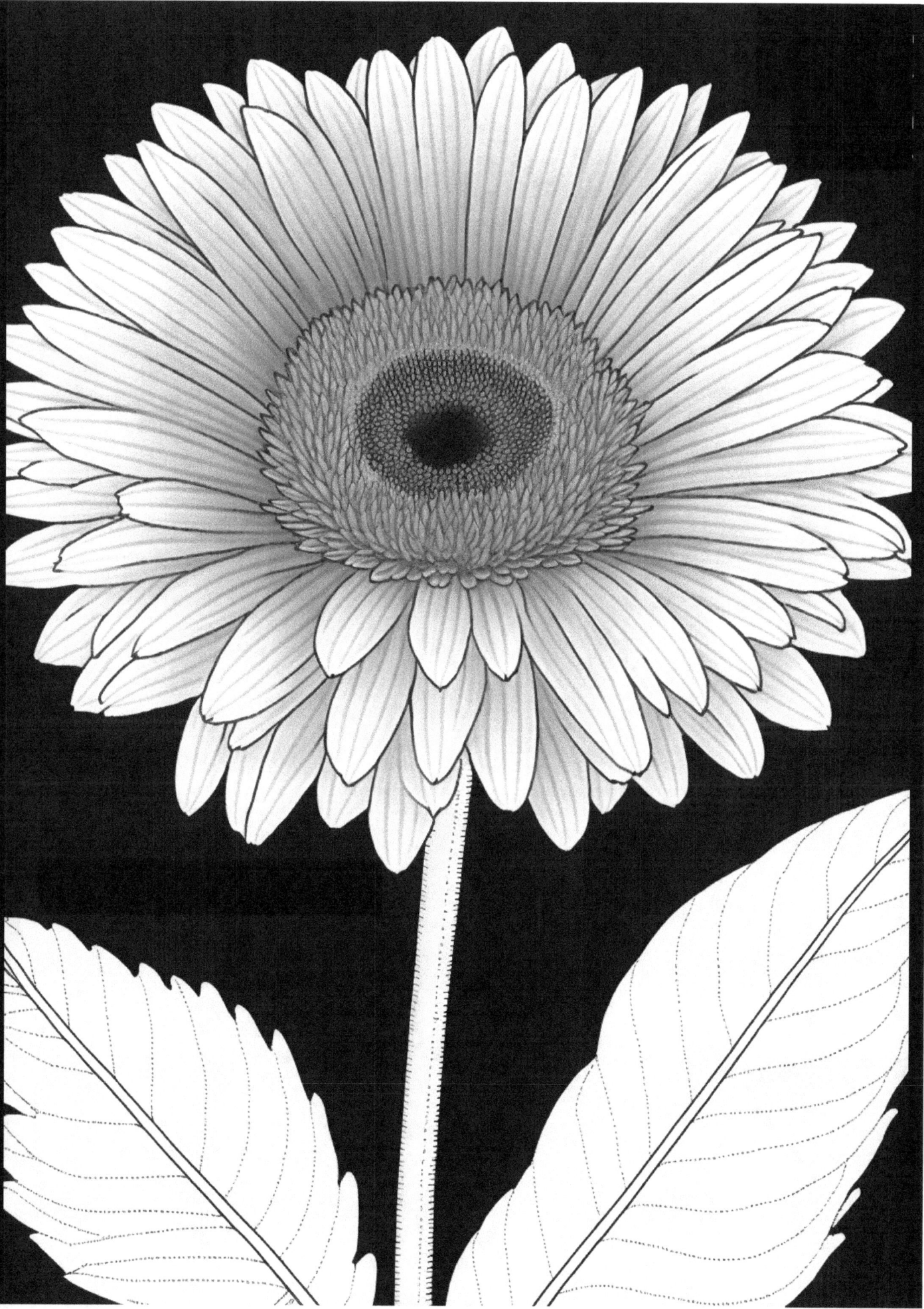

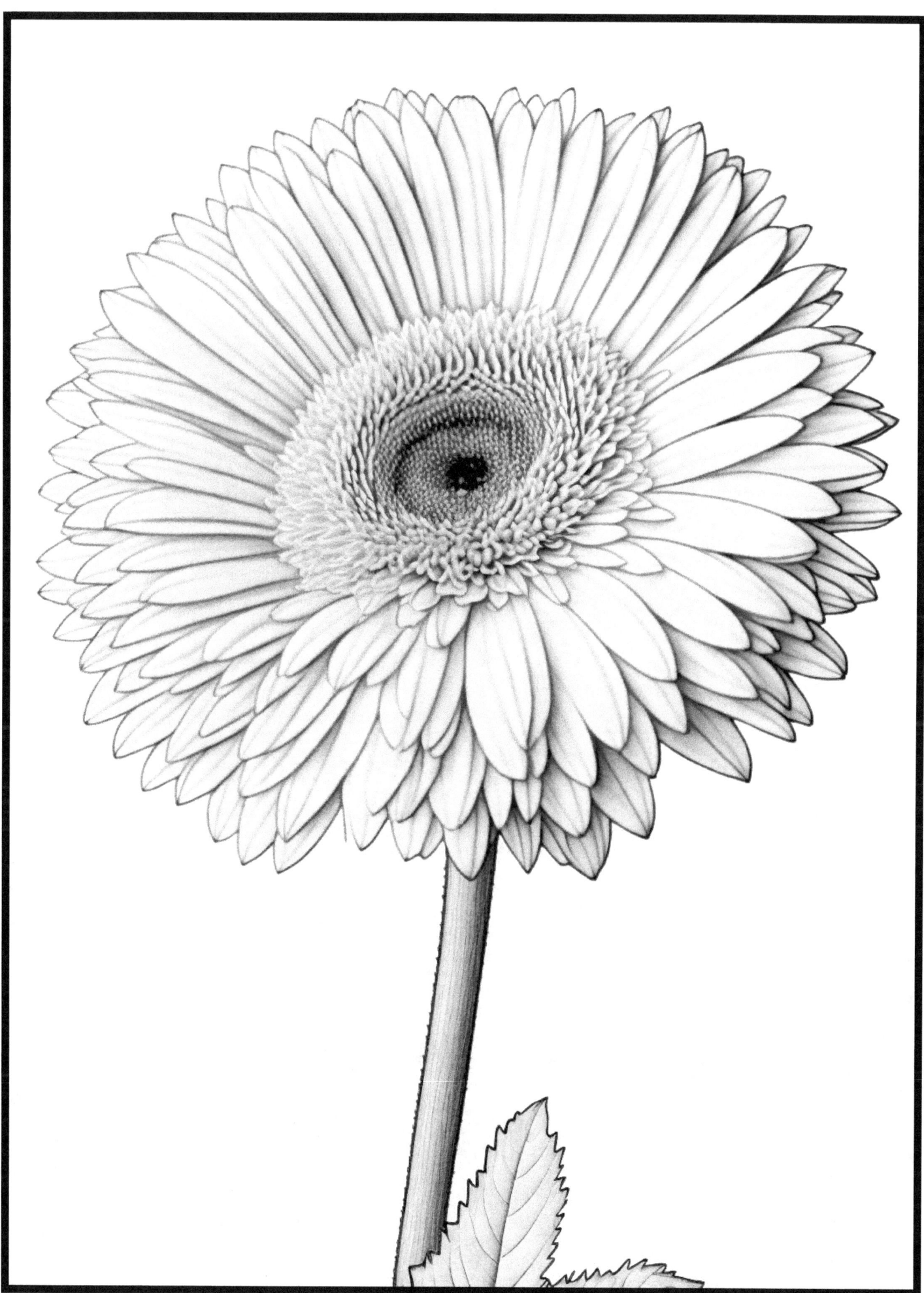

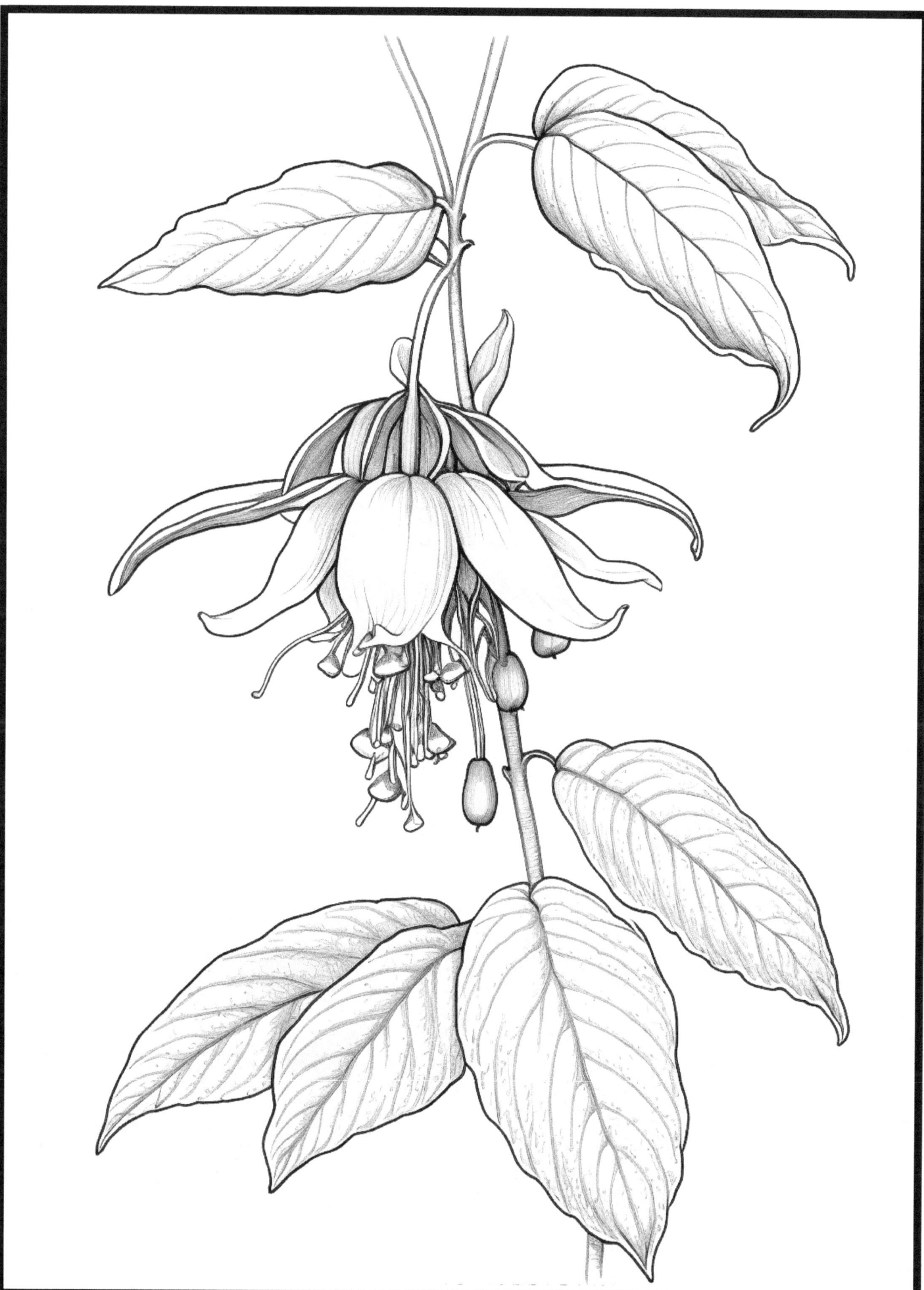

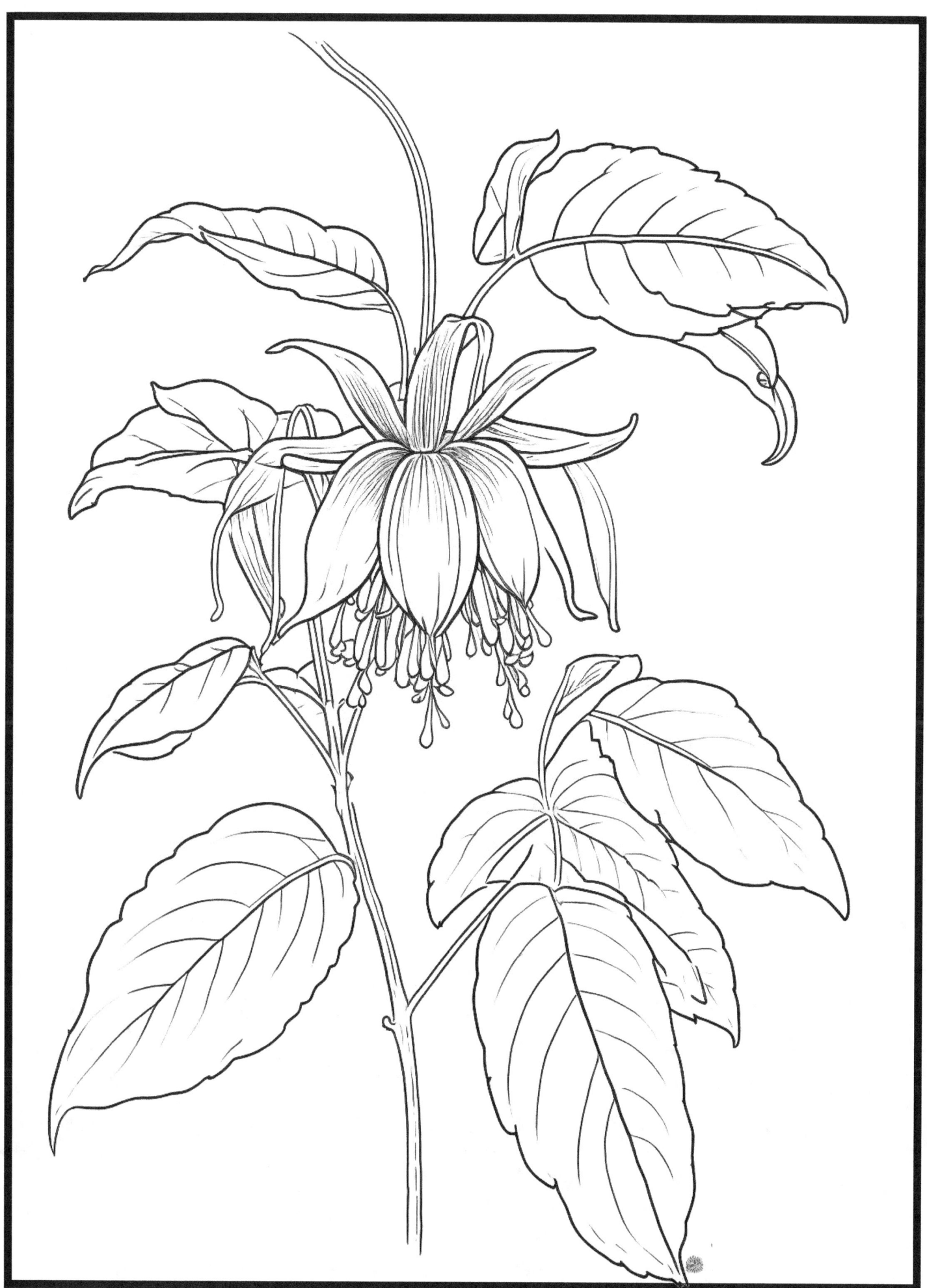

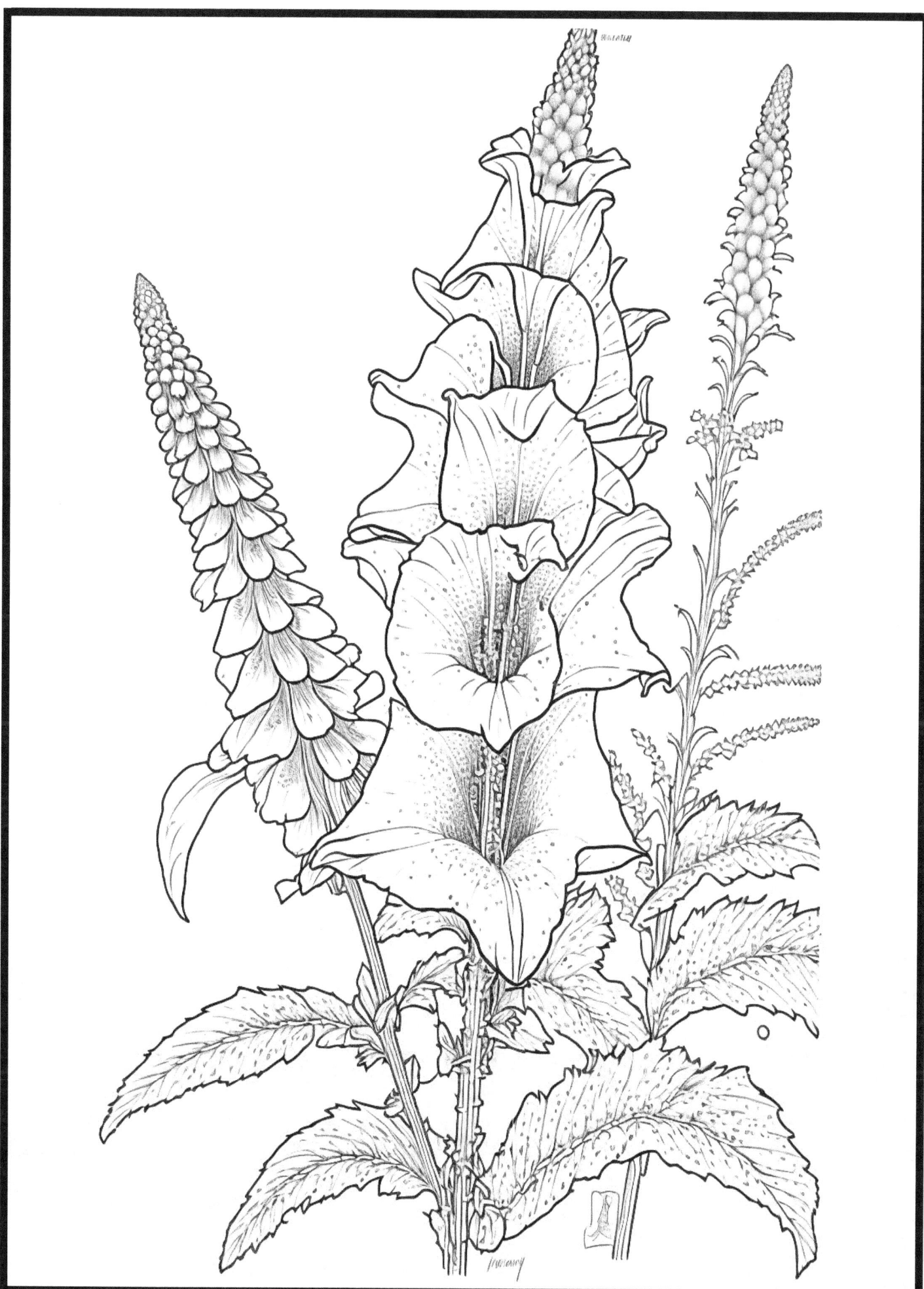

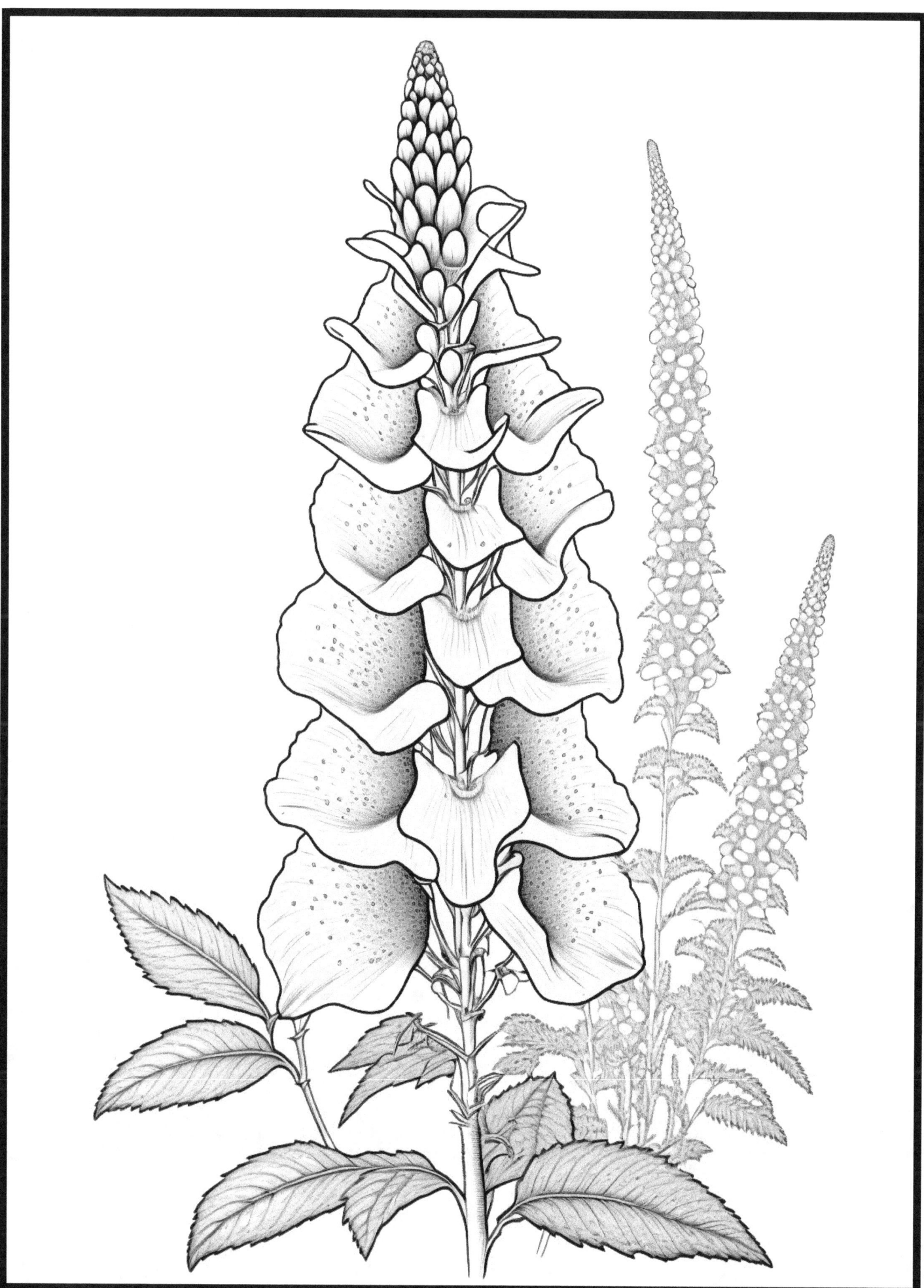

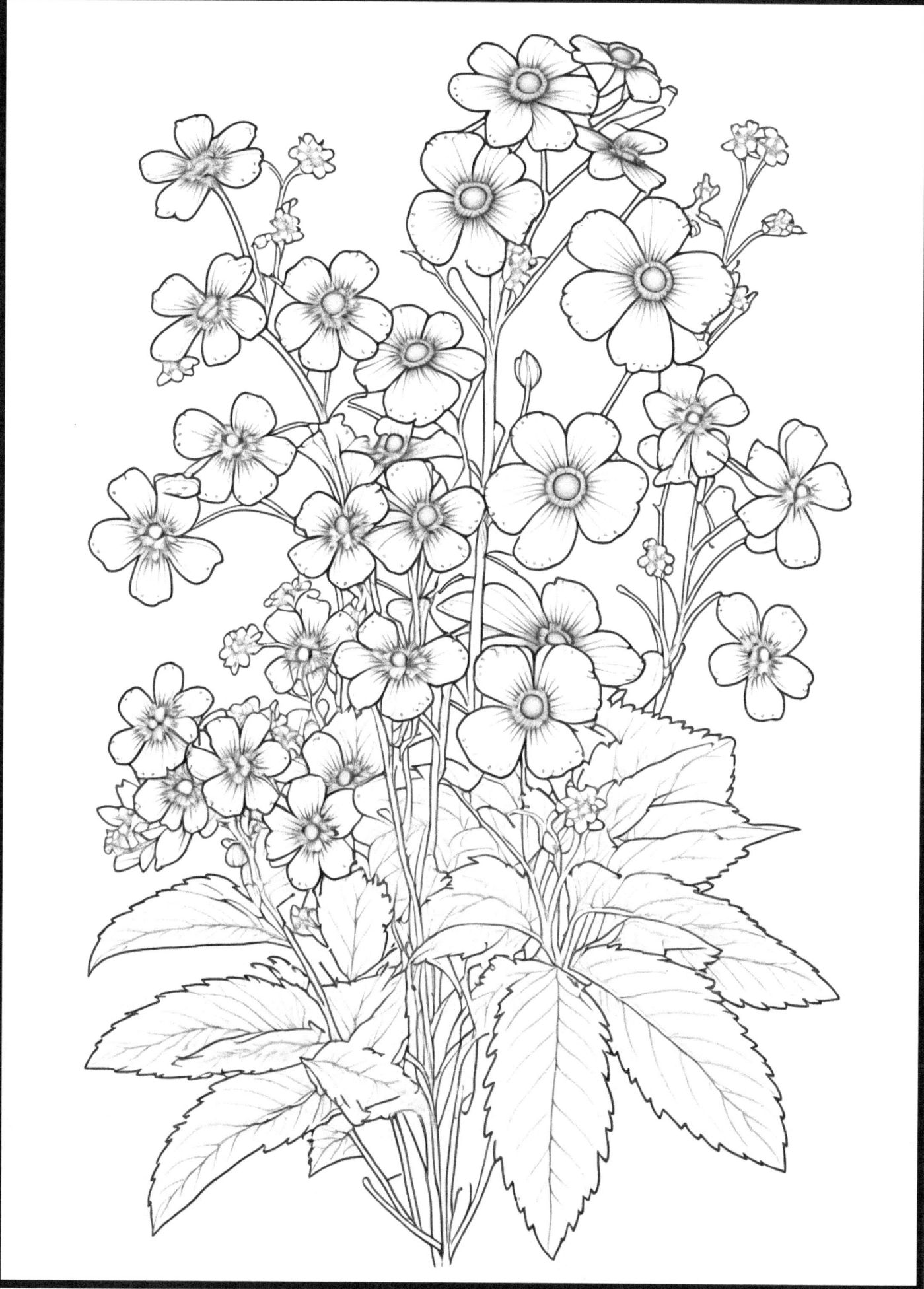

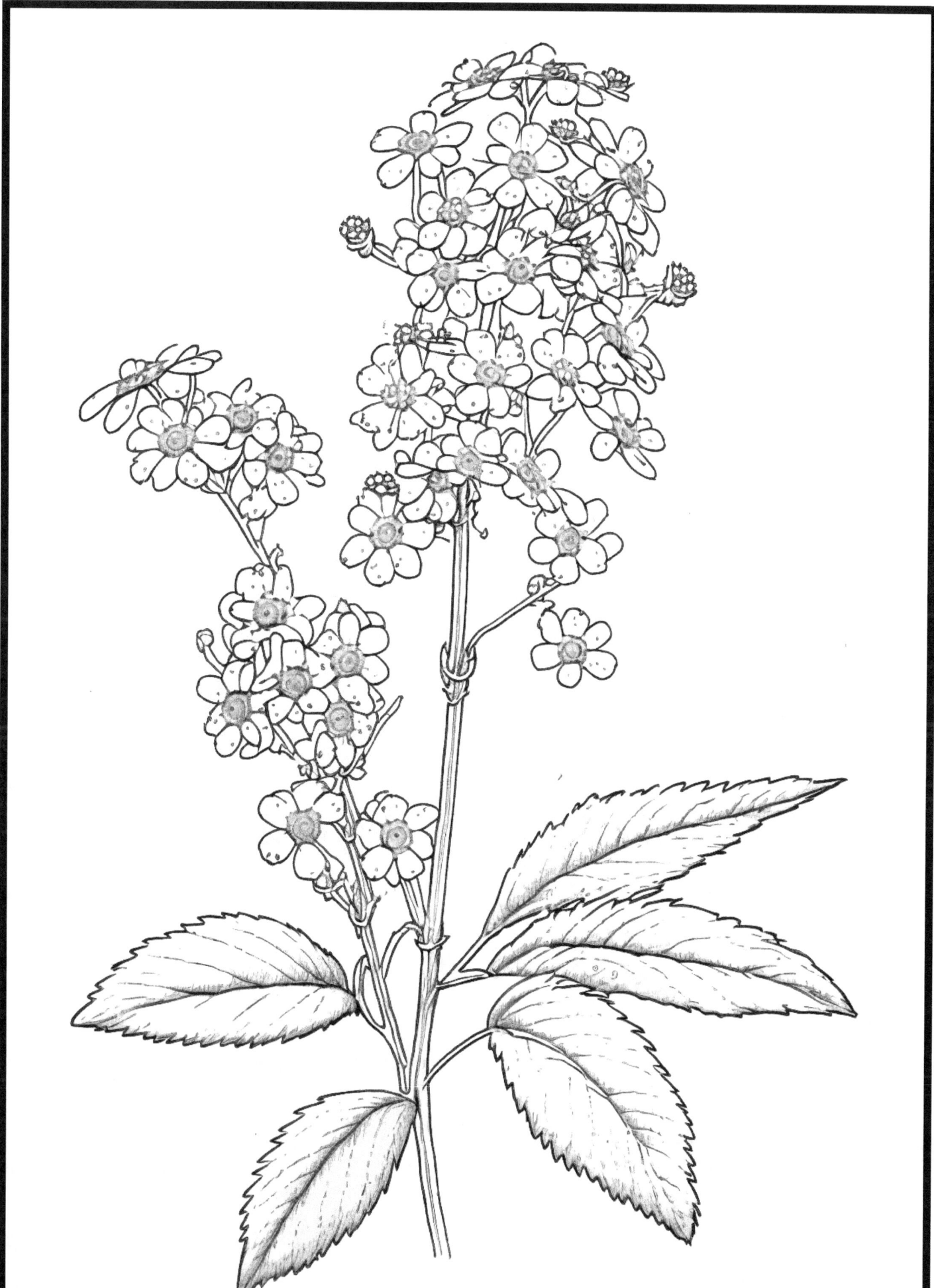

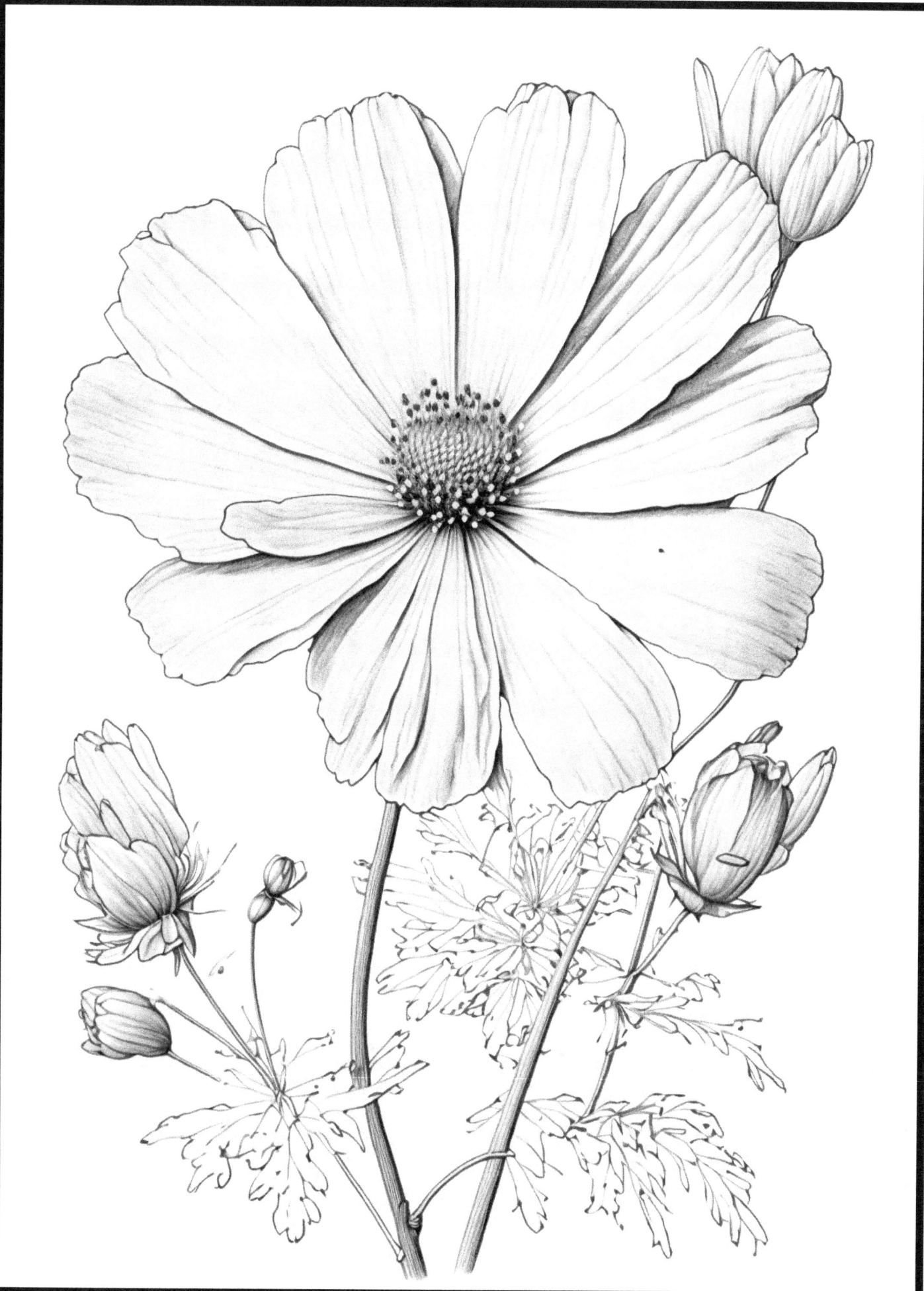

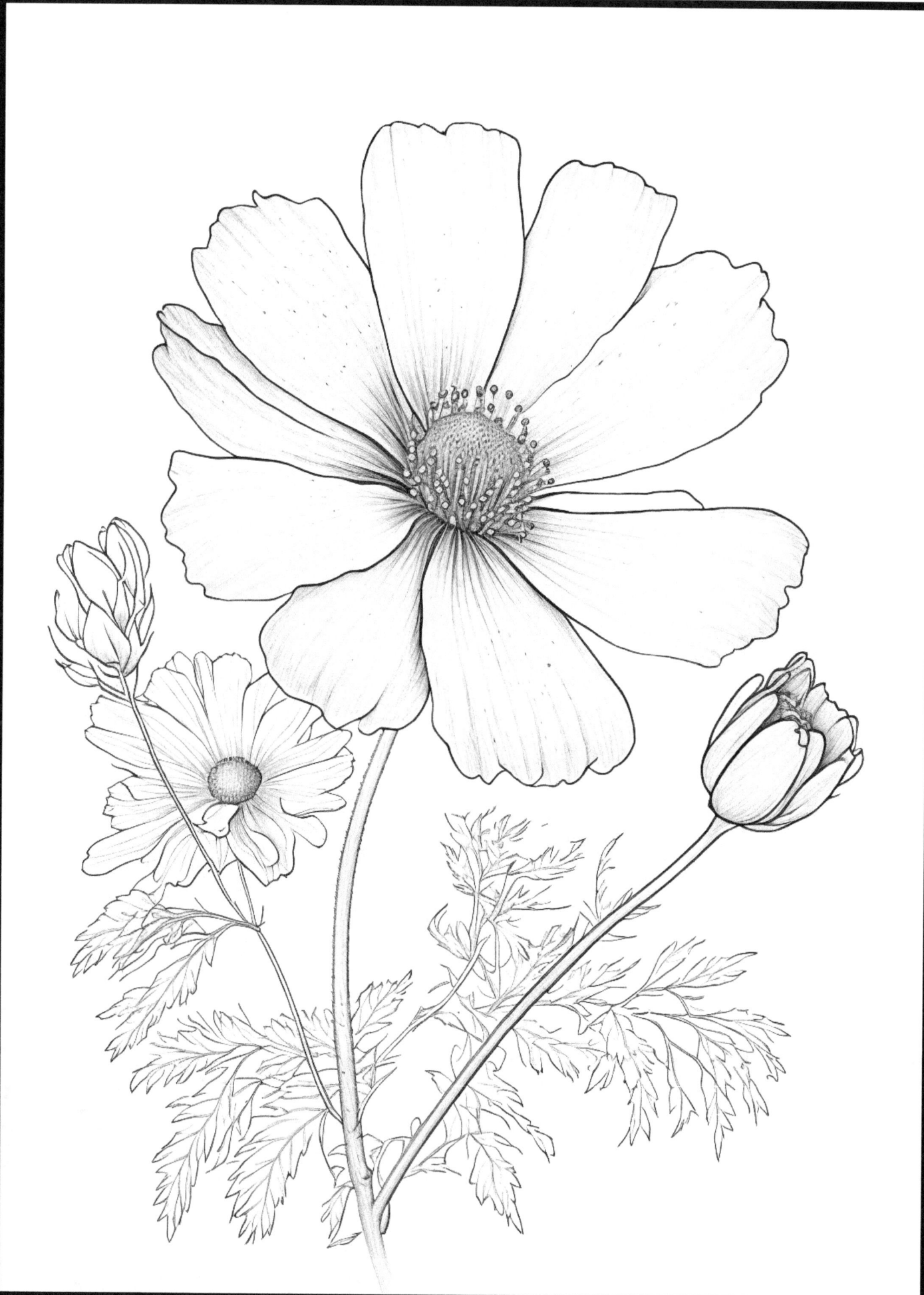

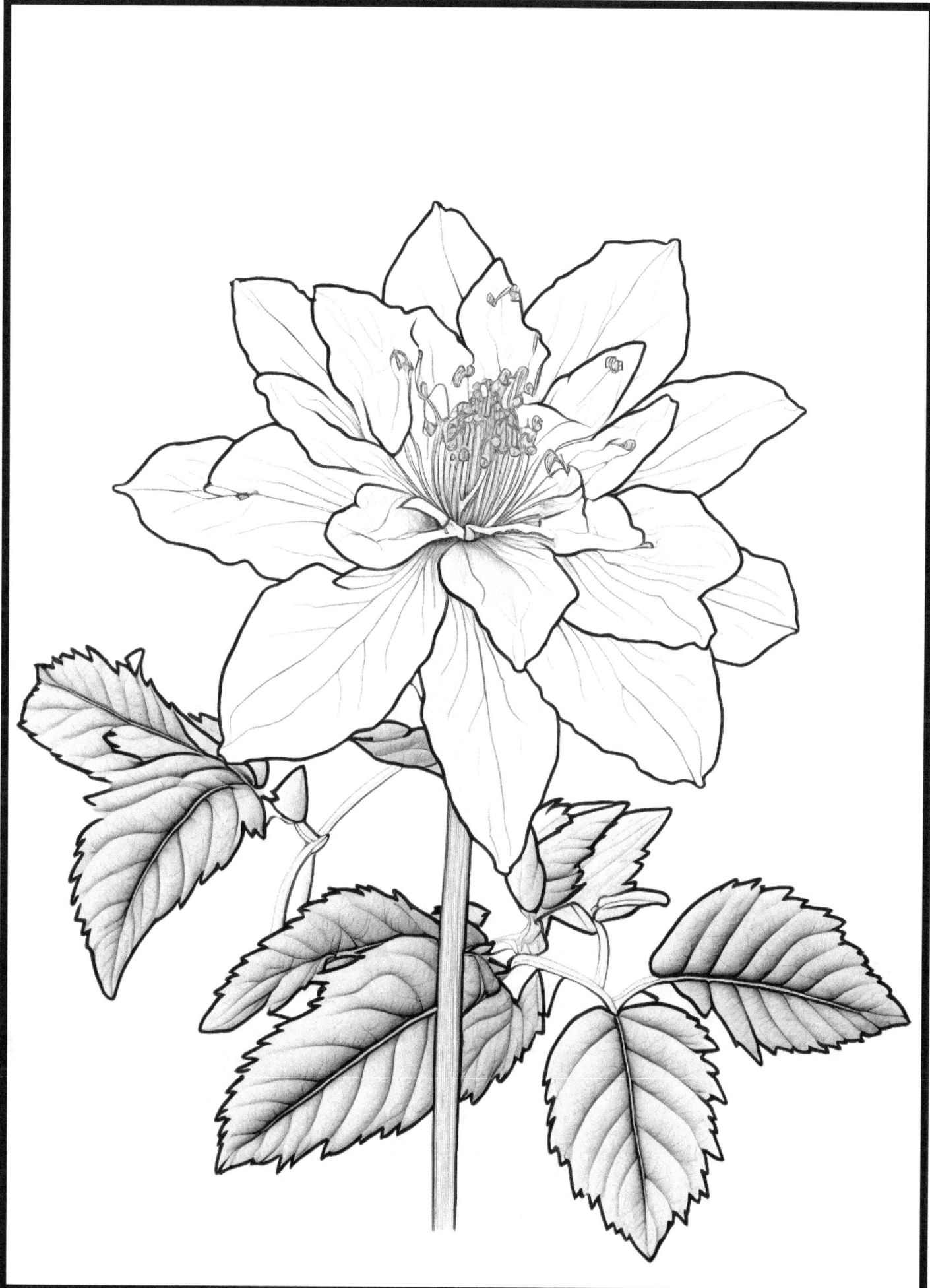

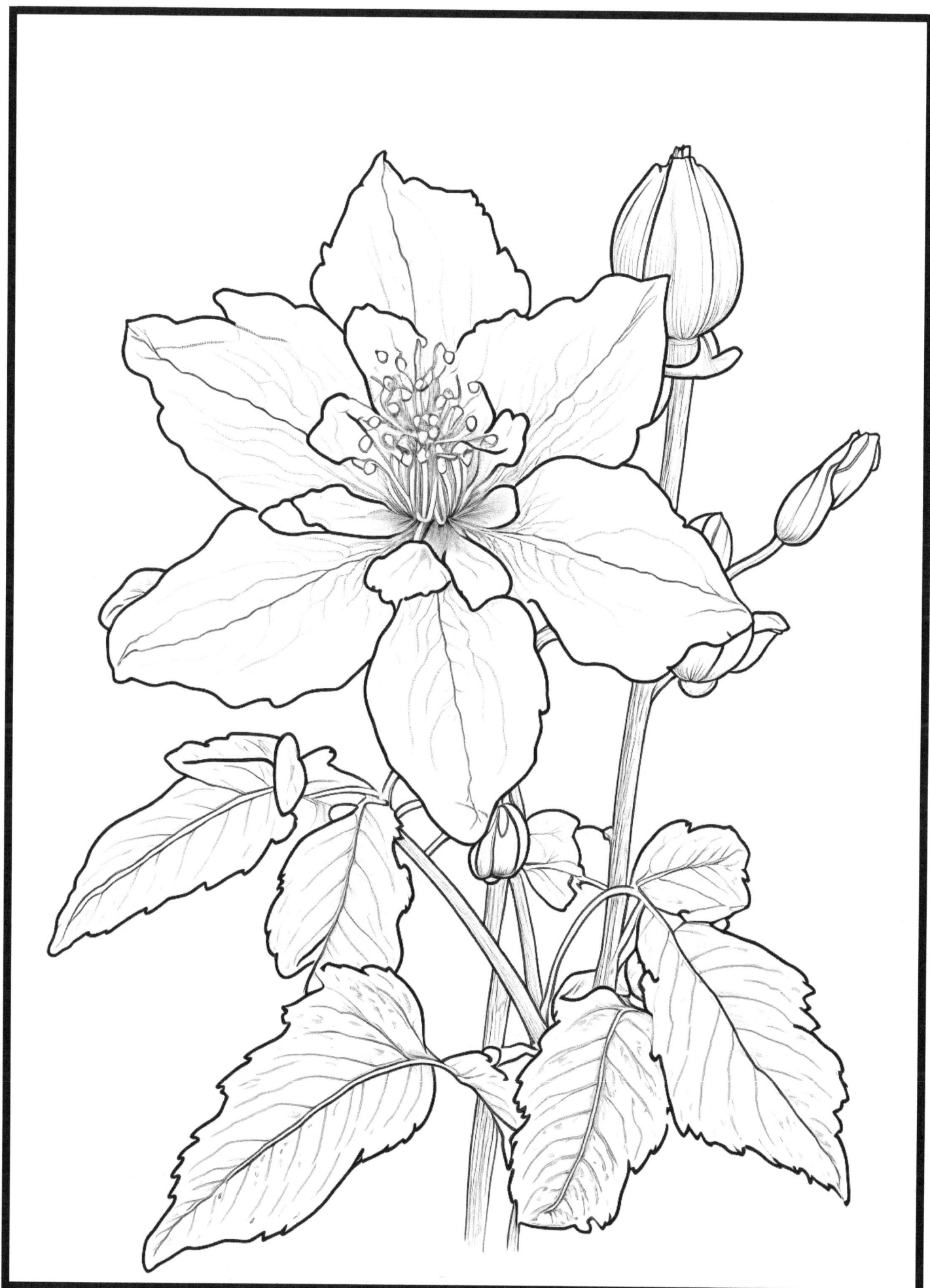

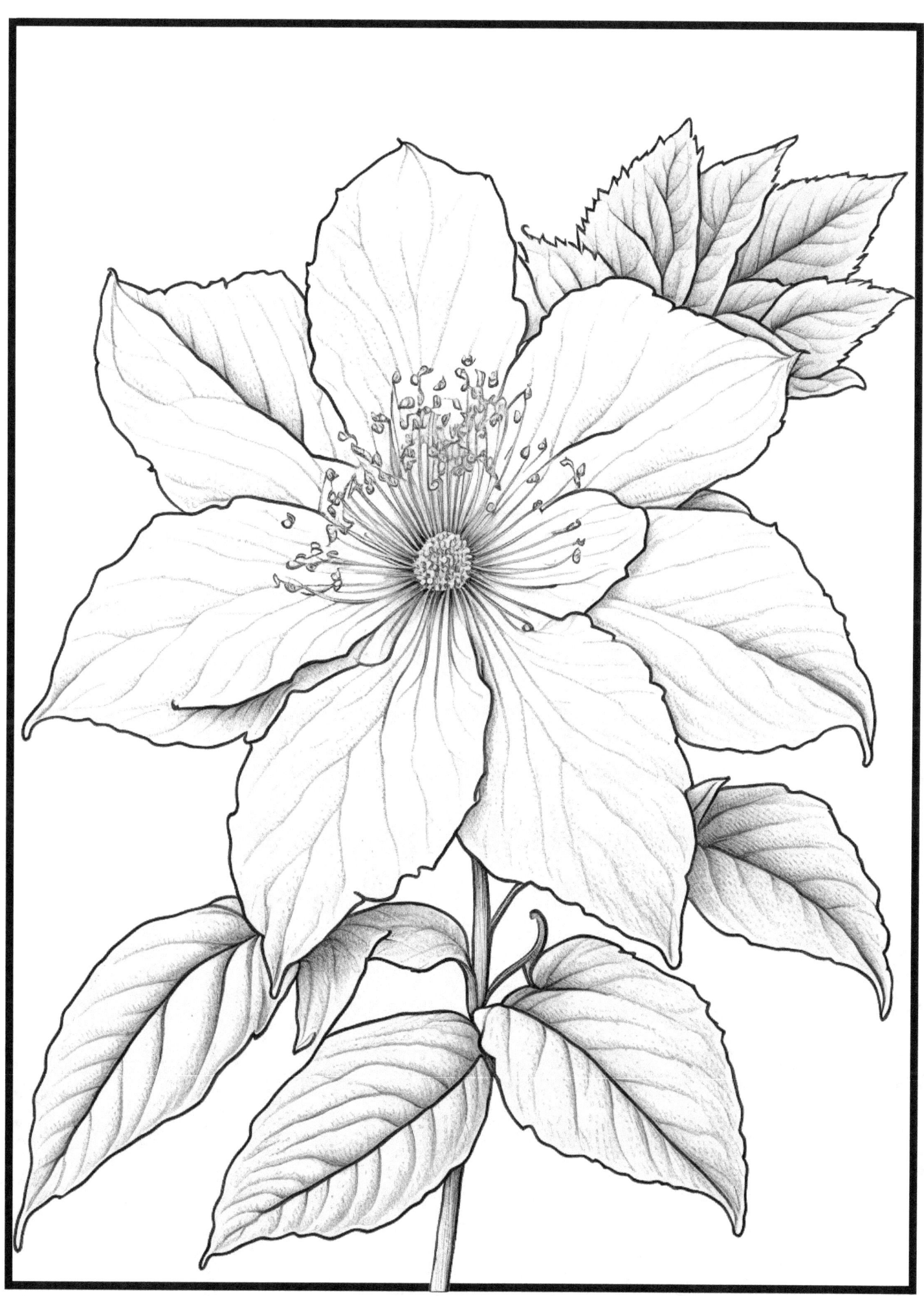

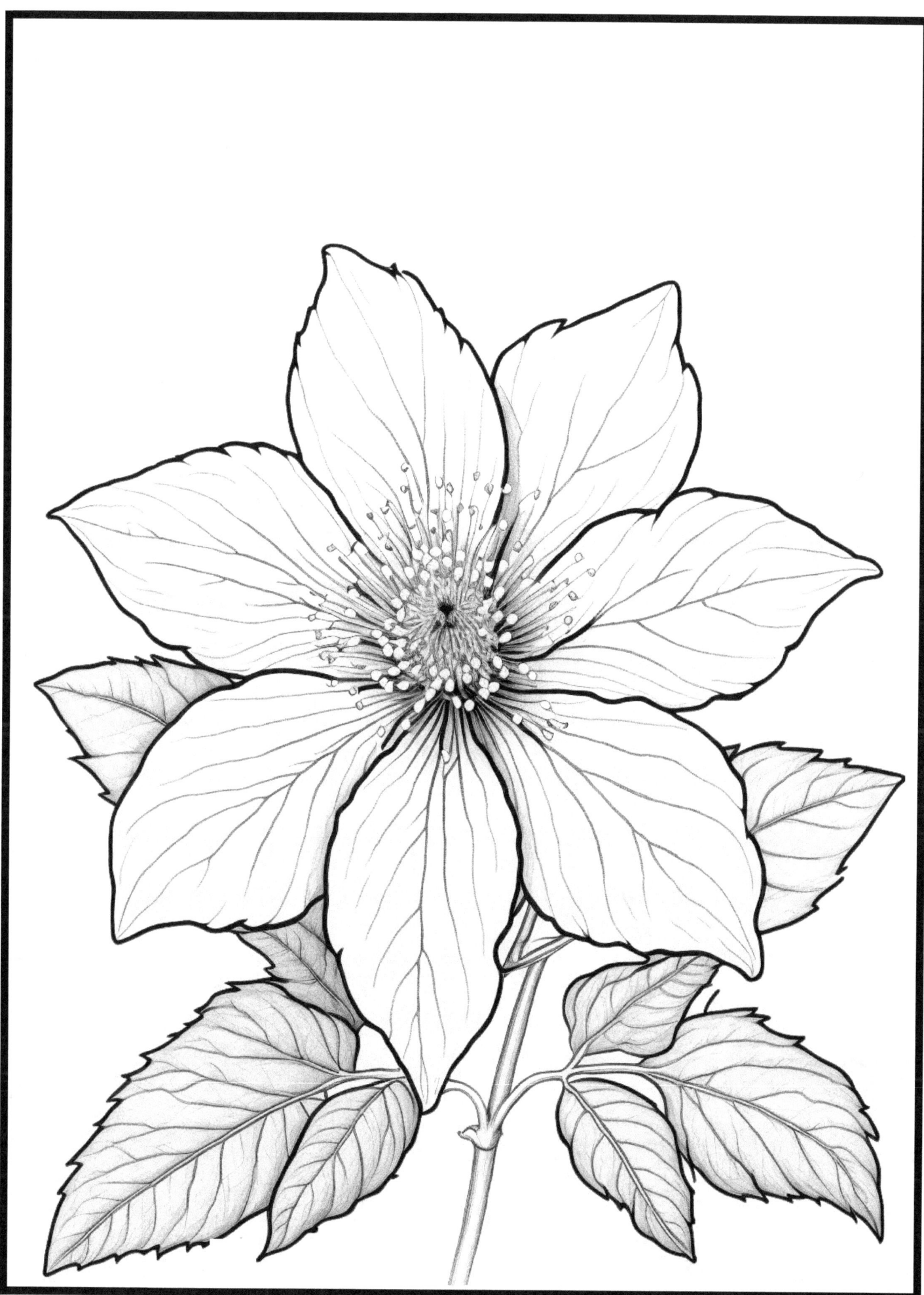

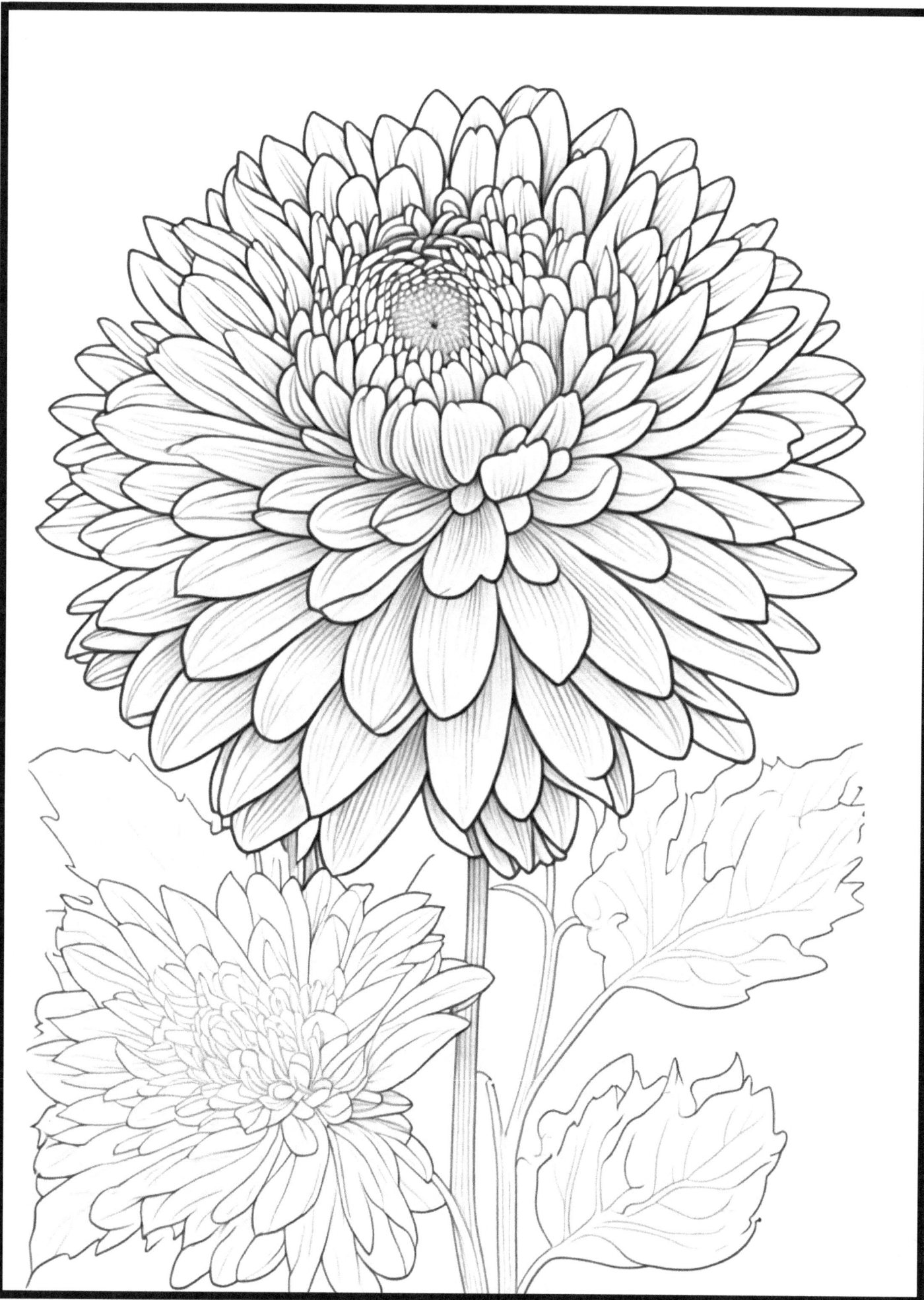

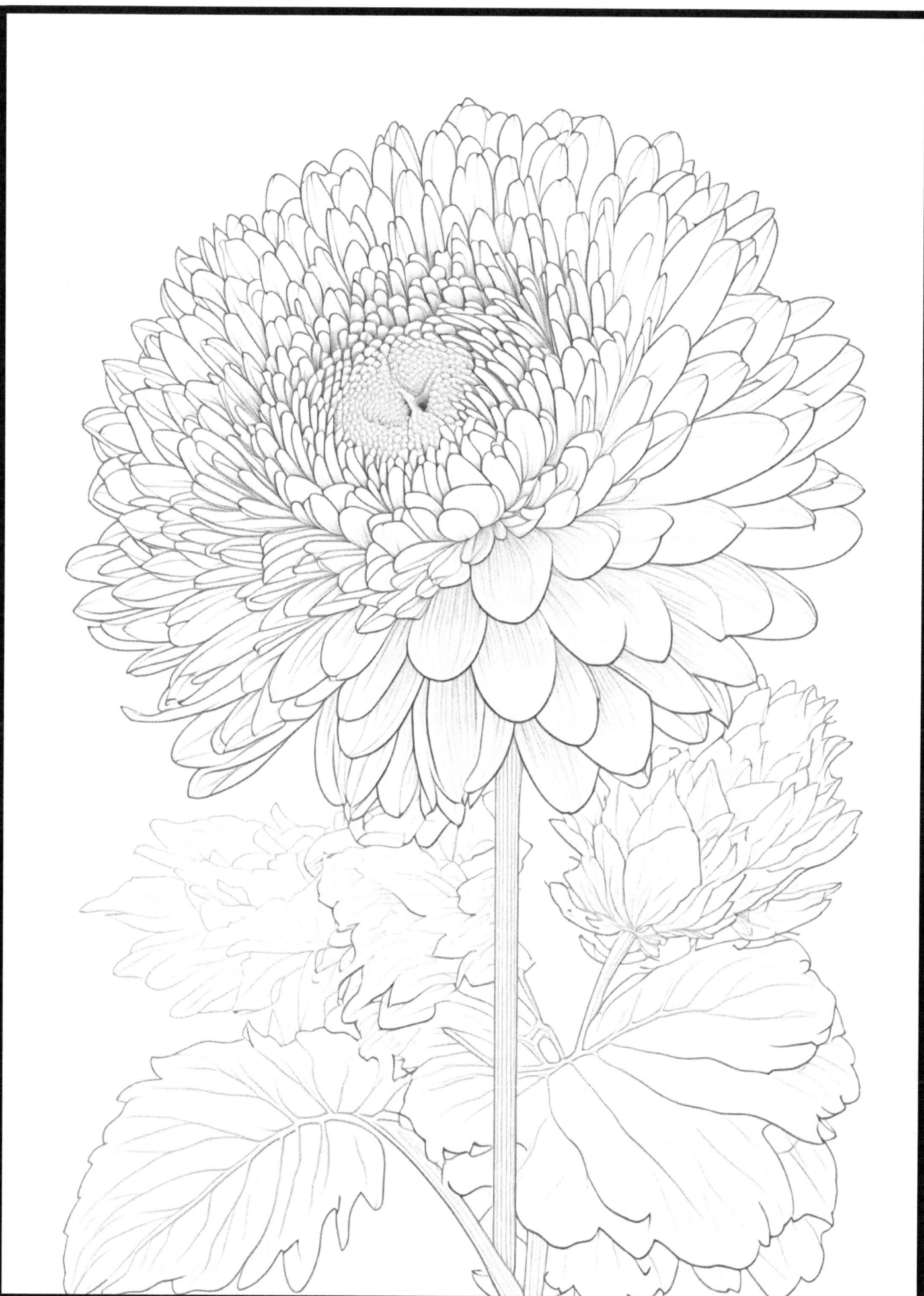

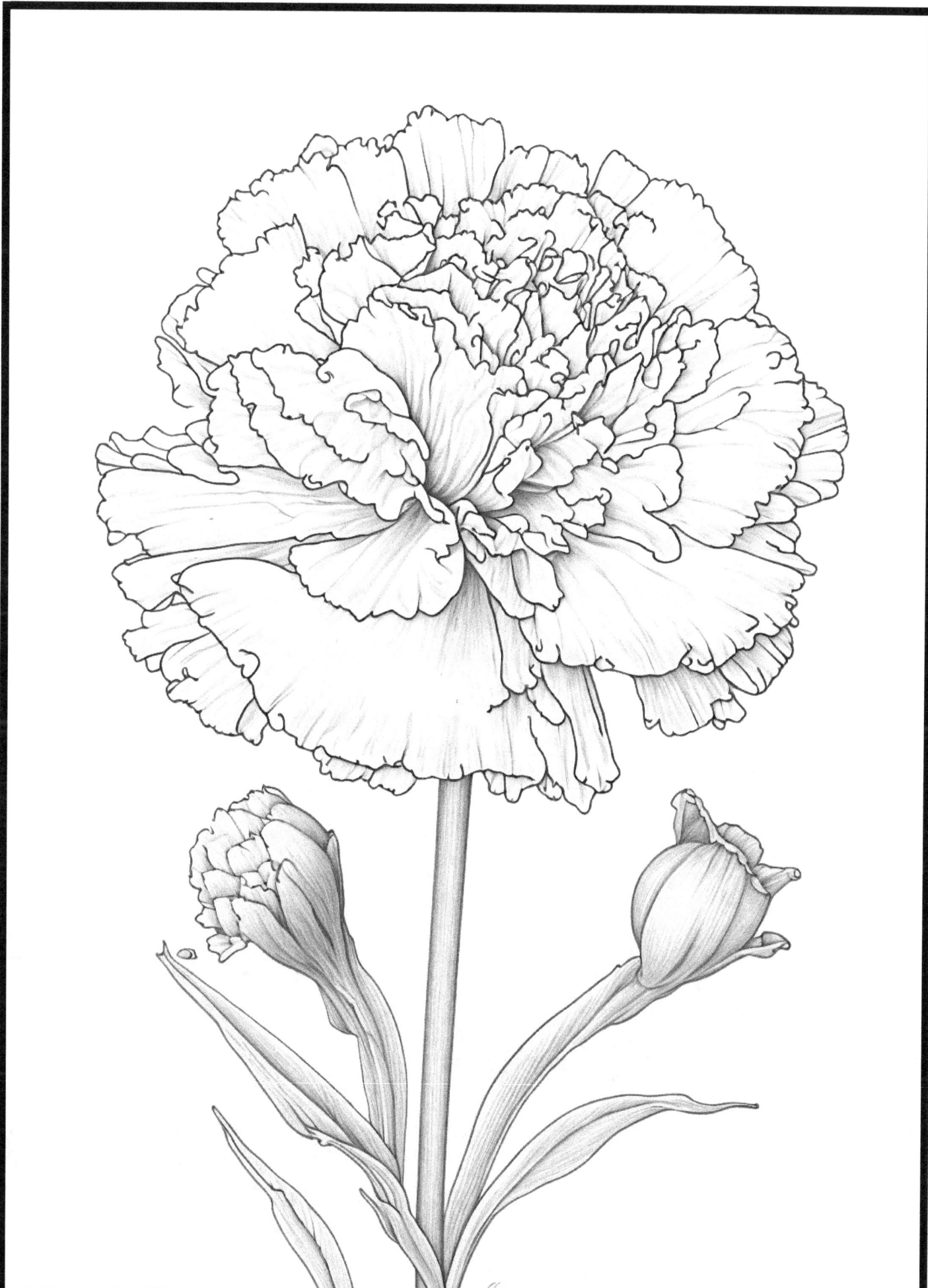

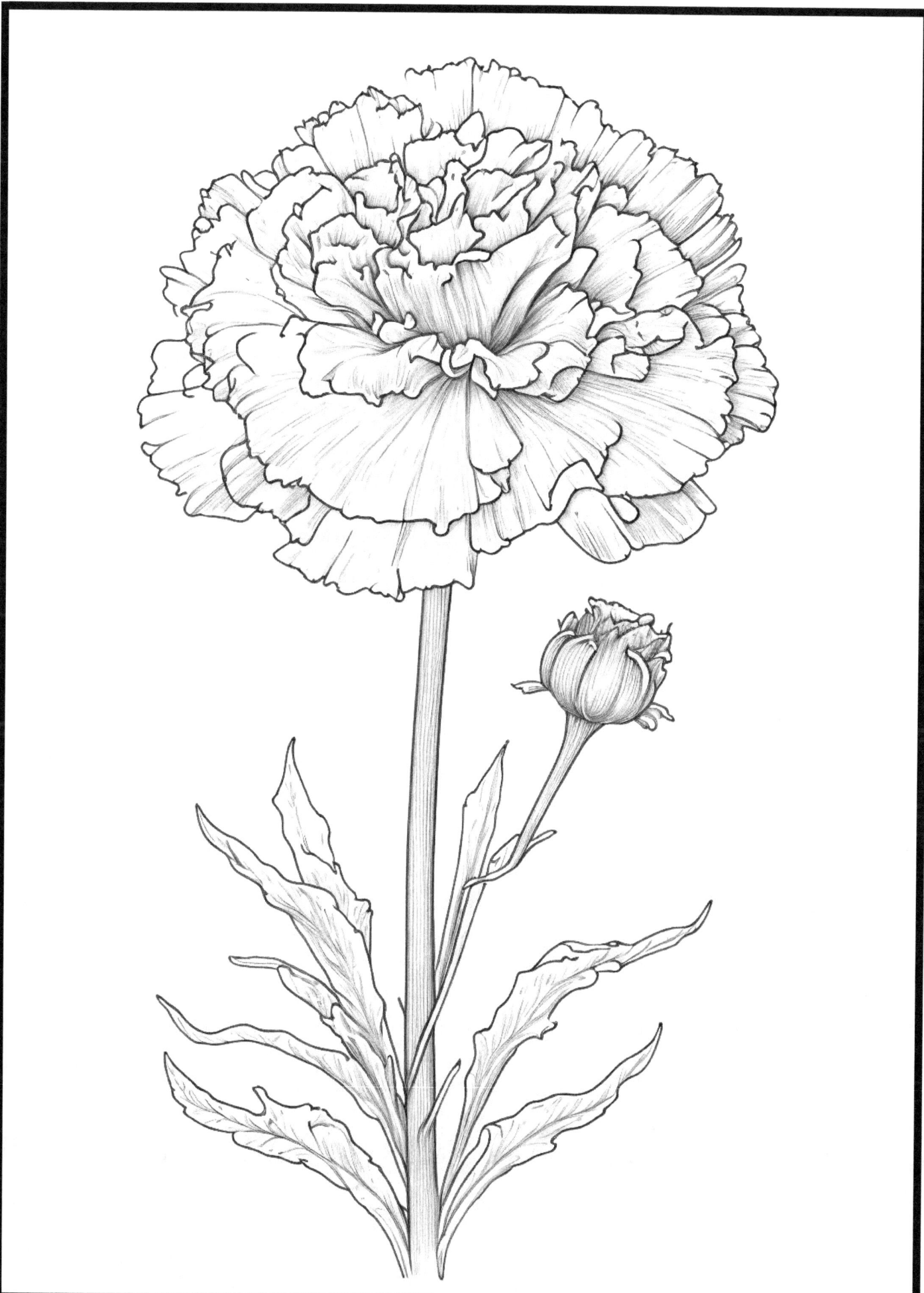

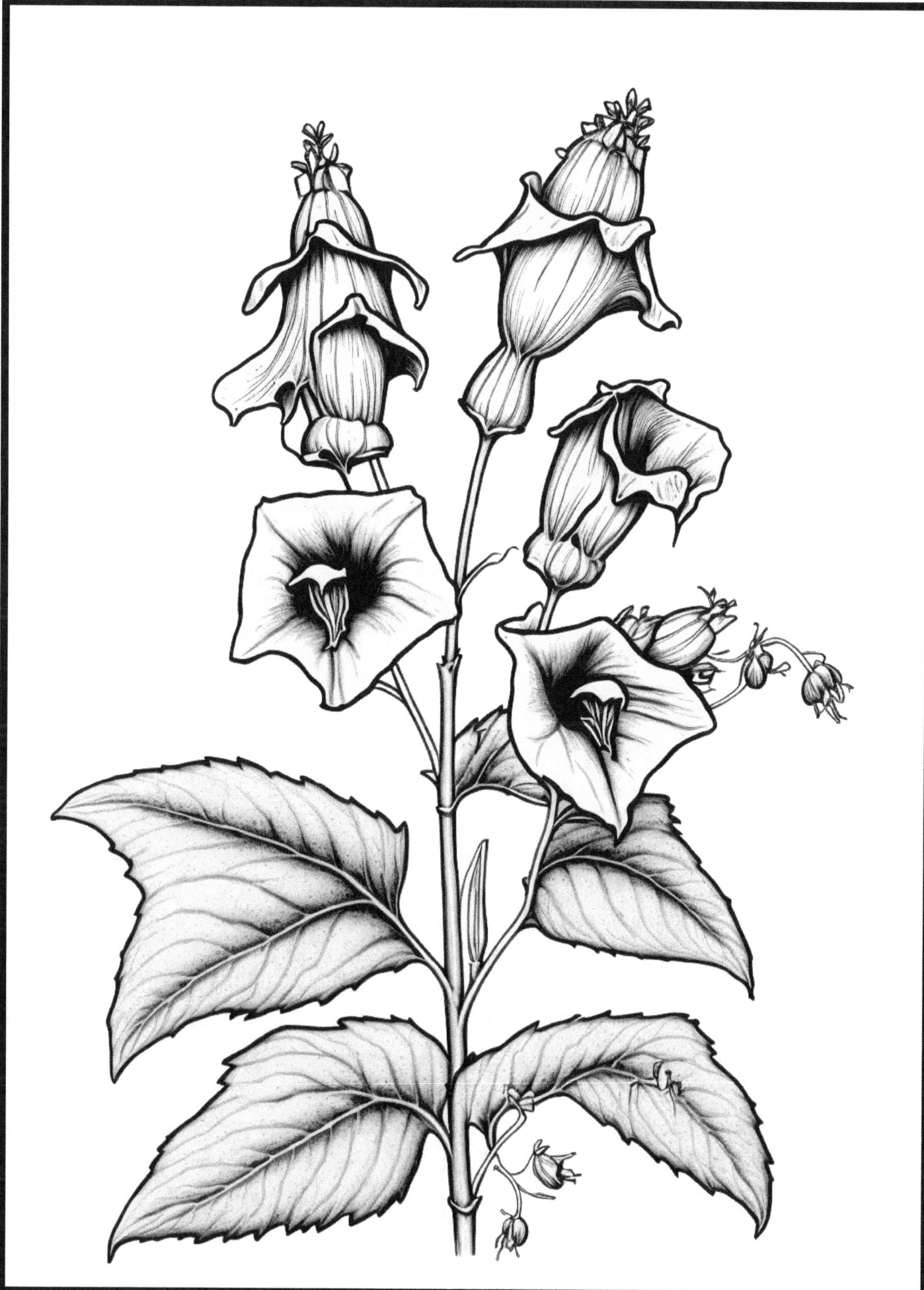

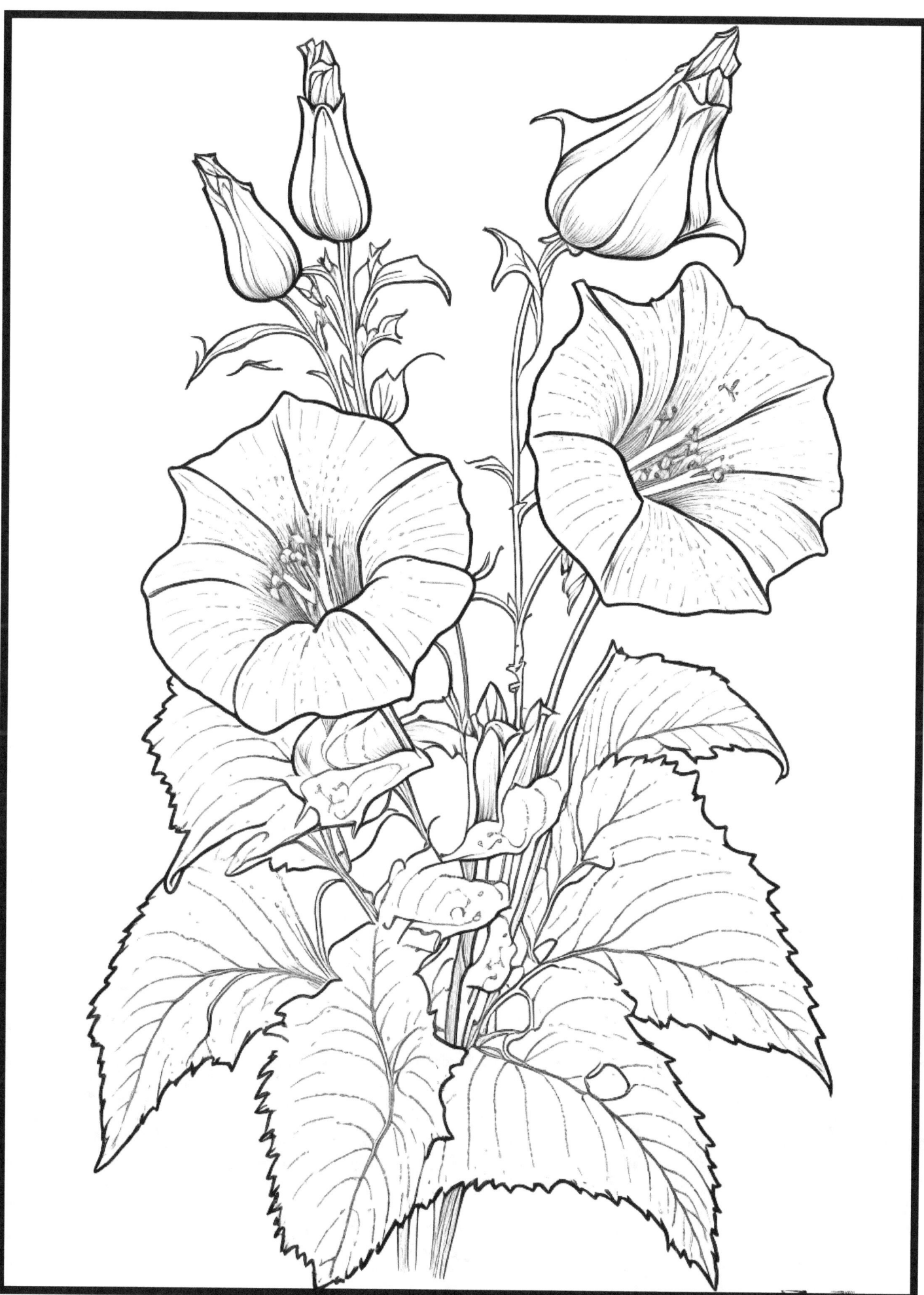

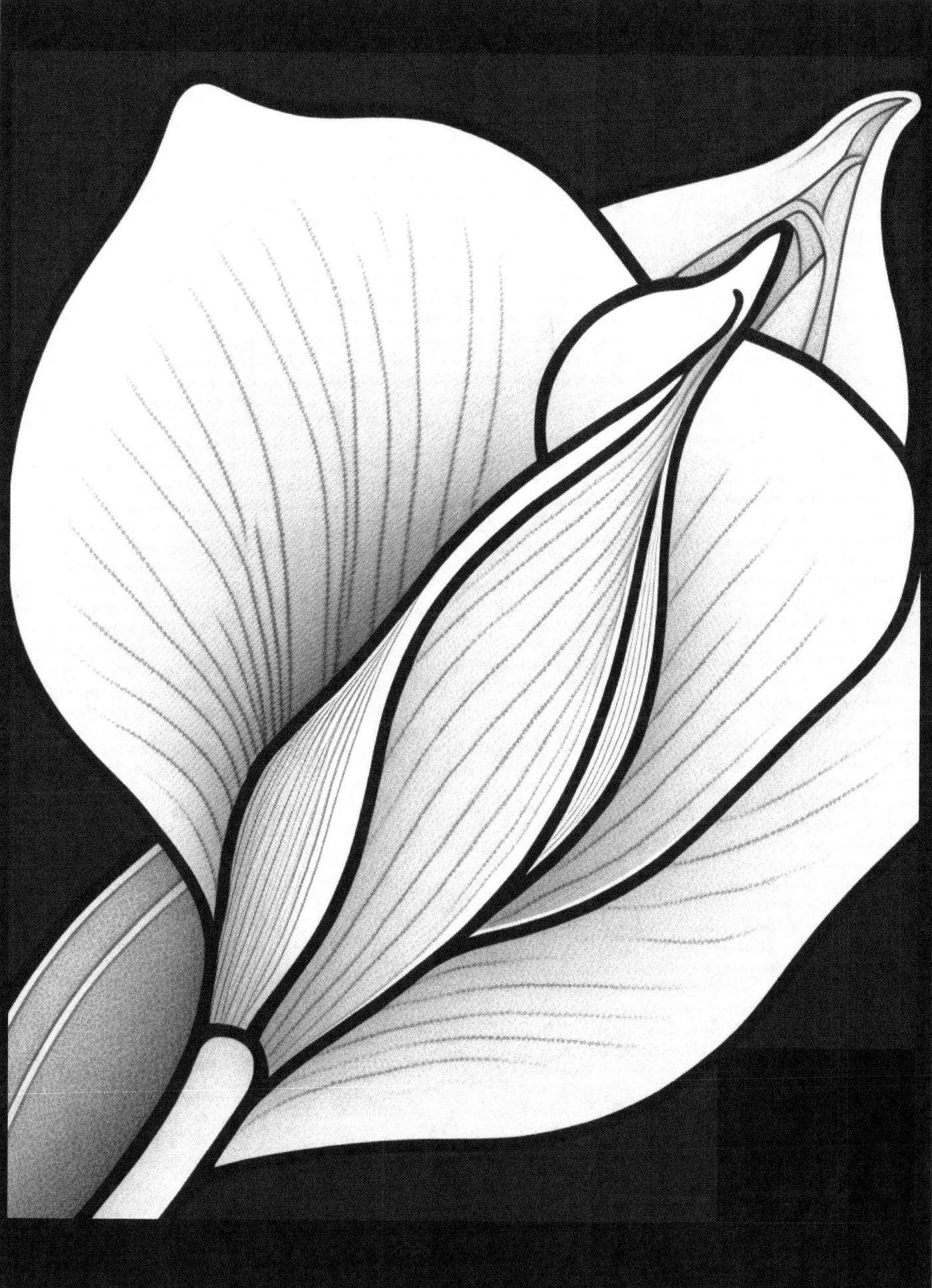

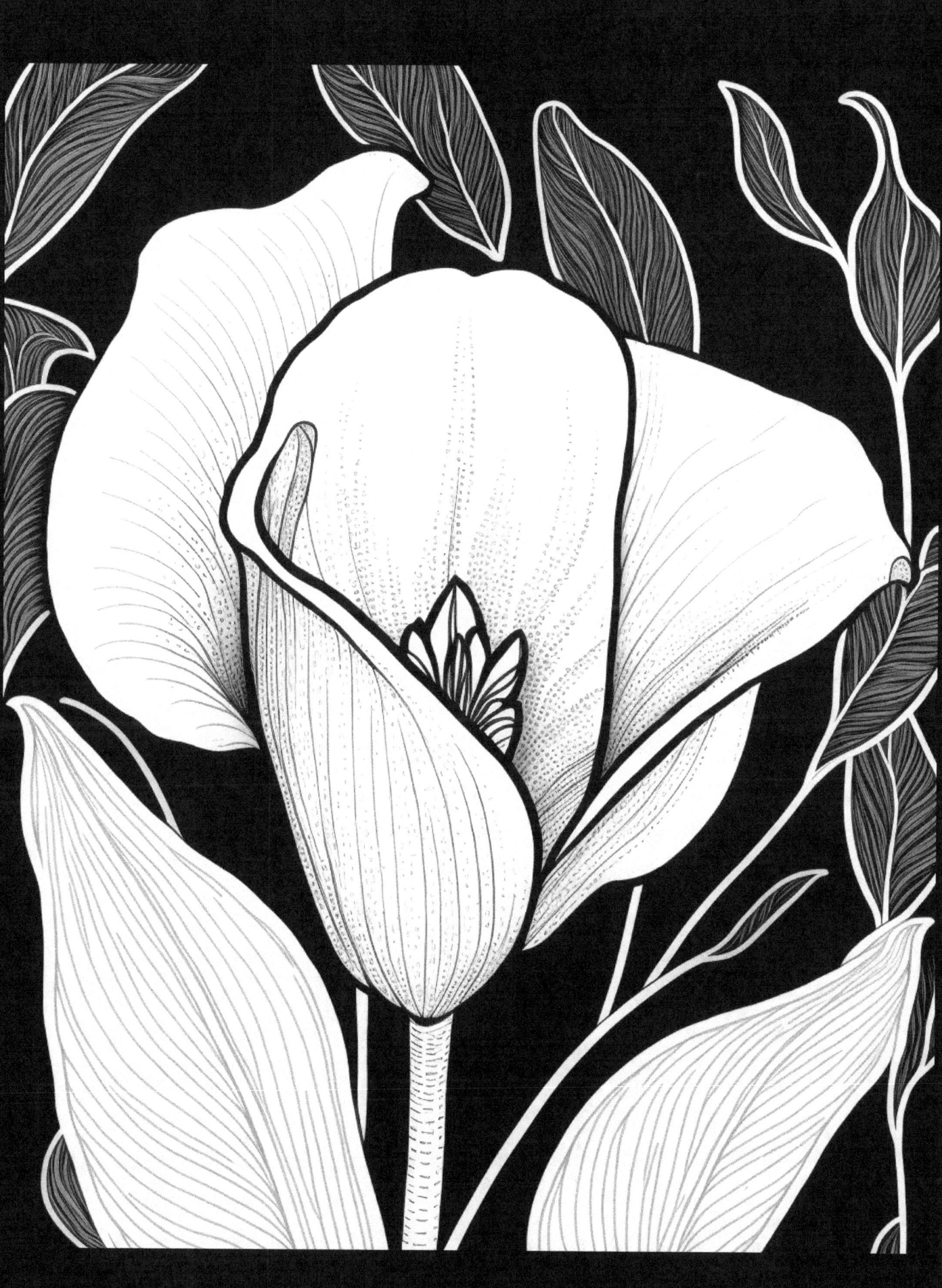

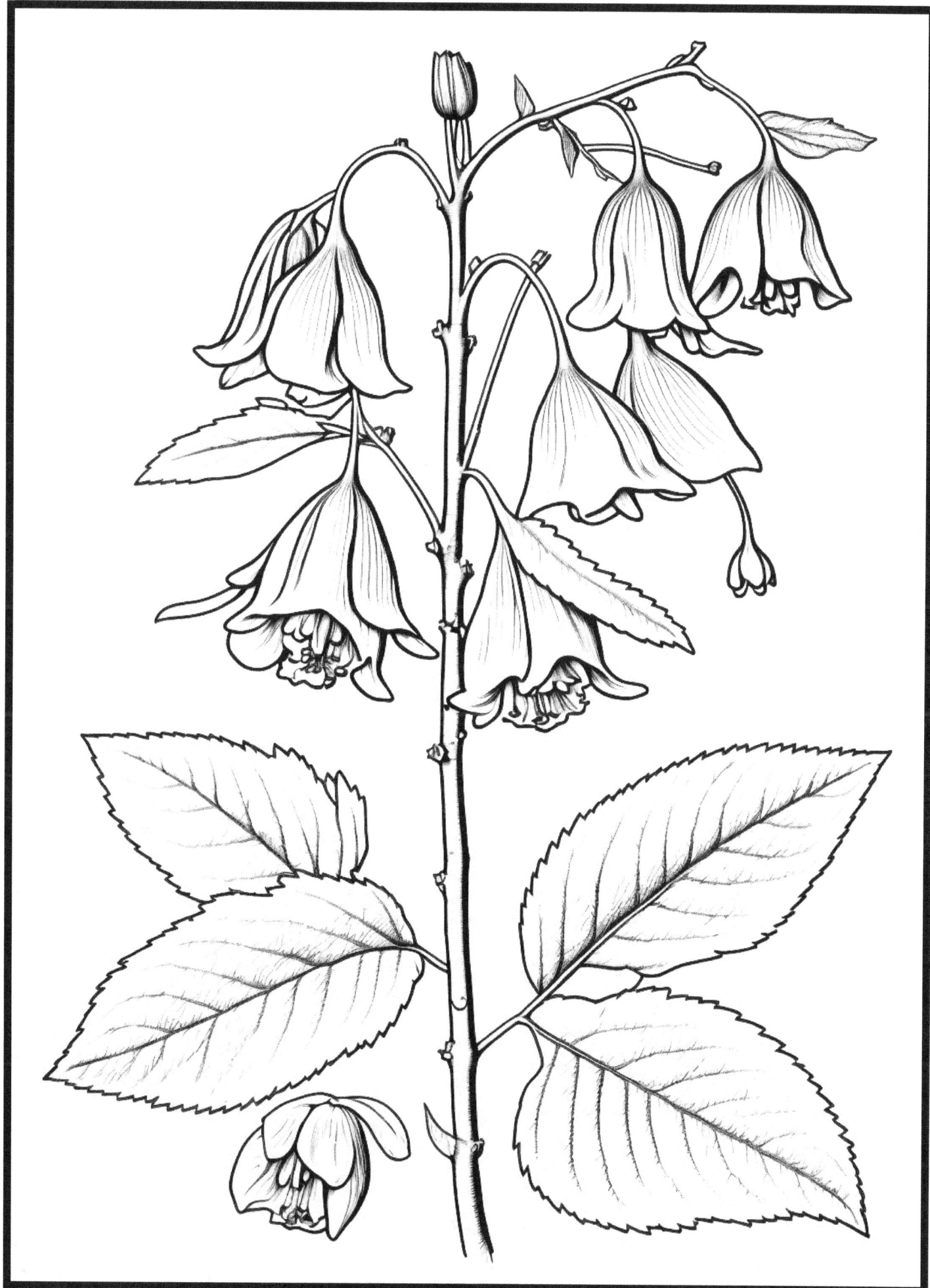

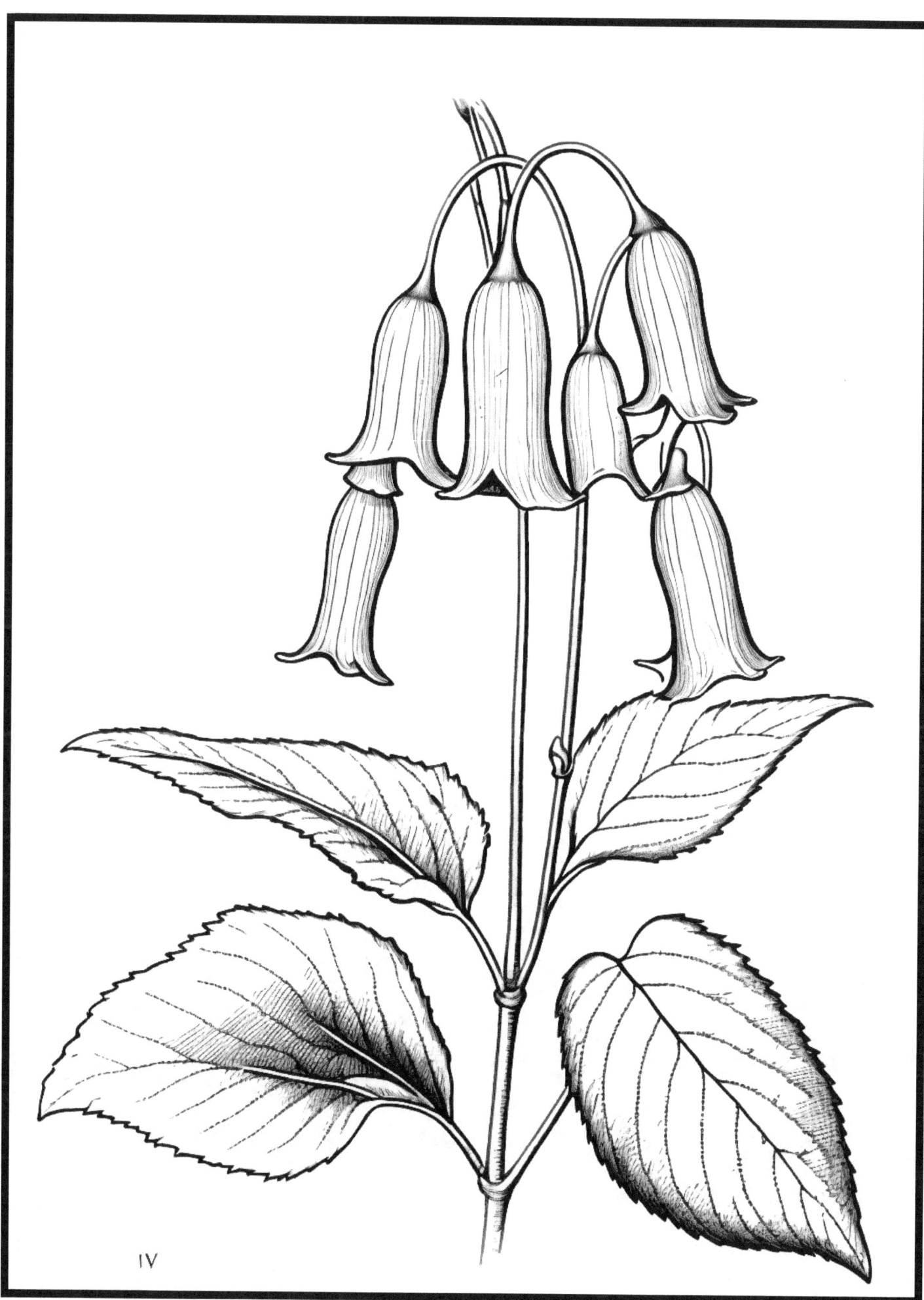

IV

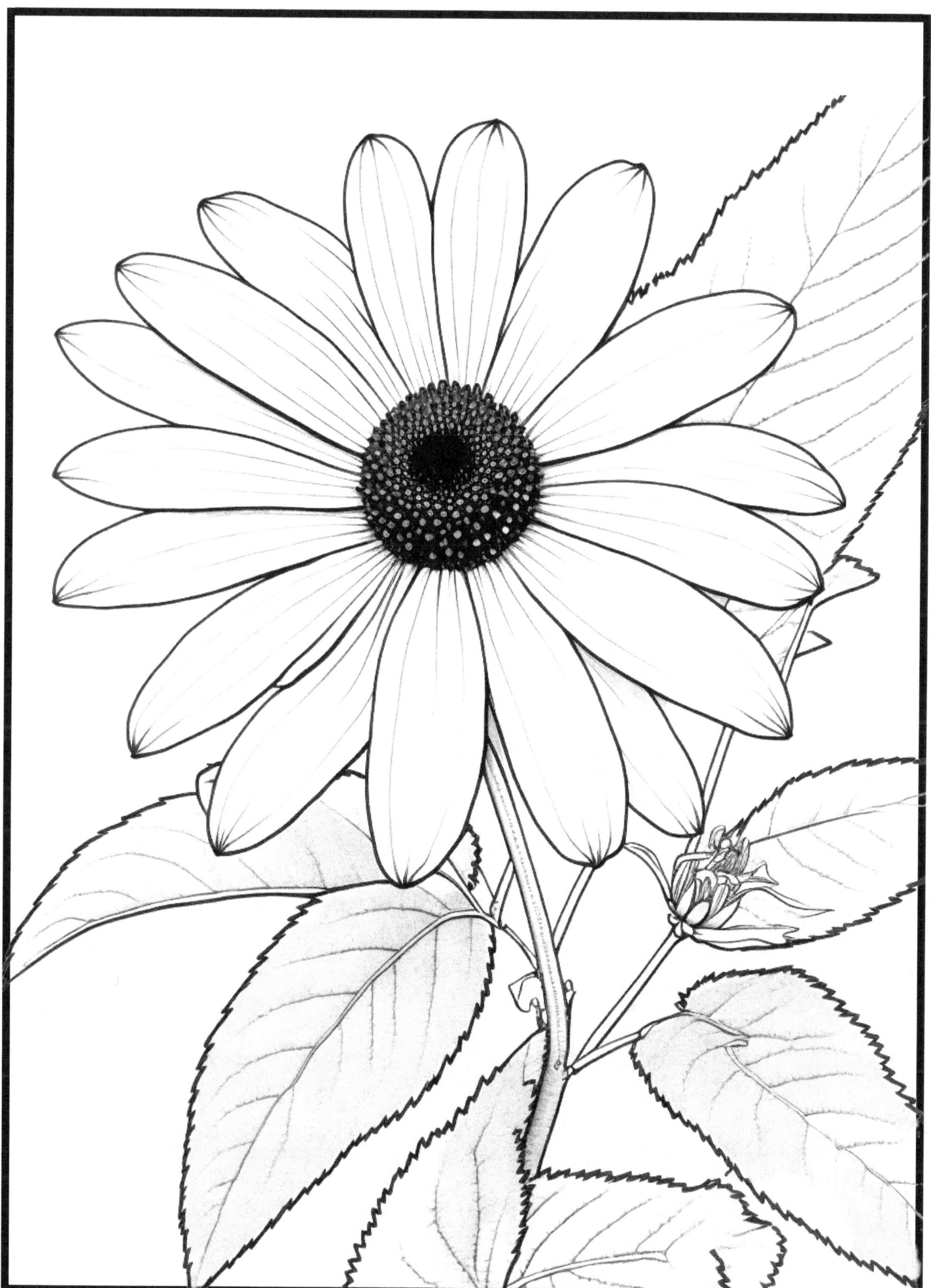

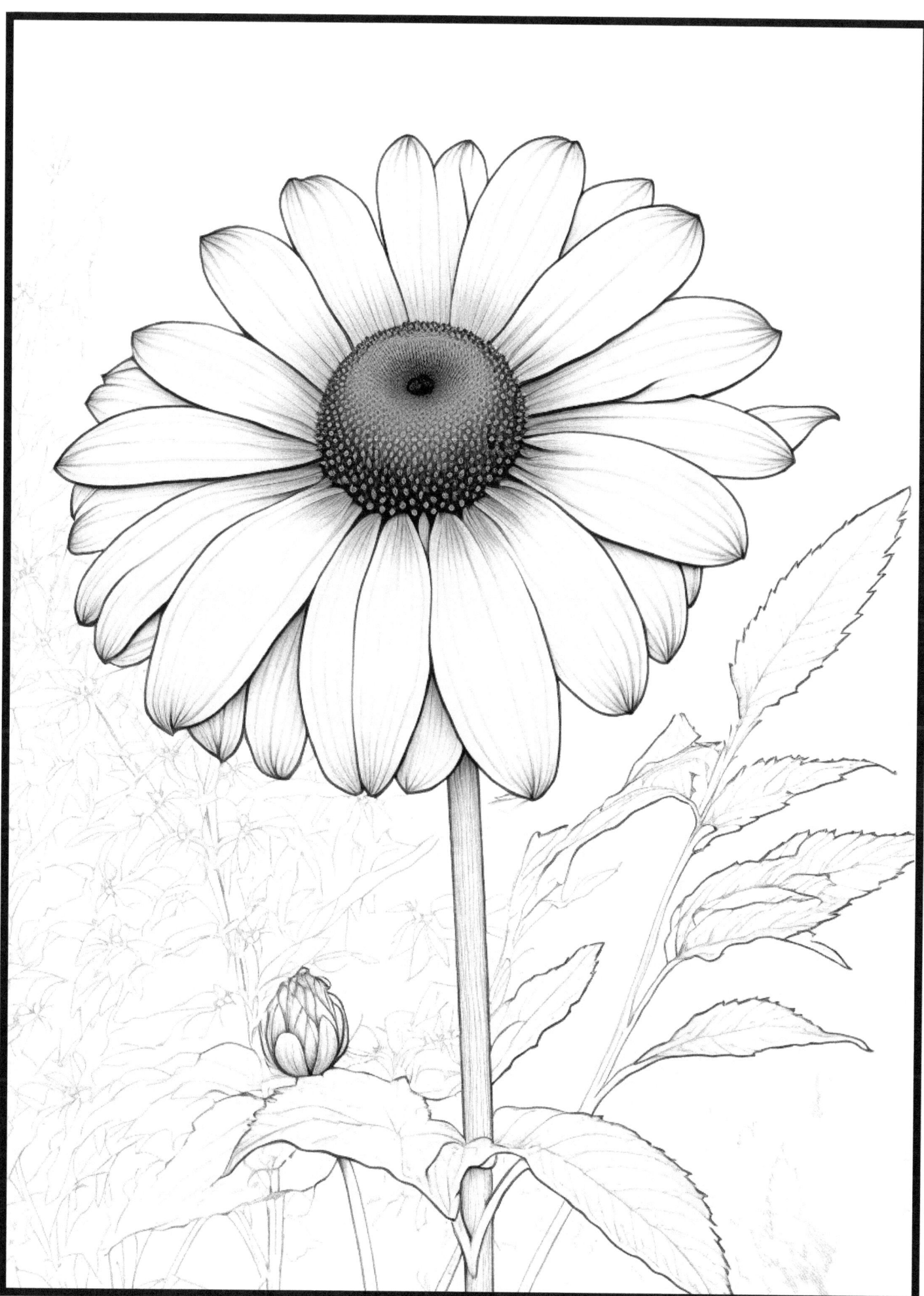

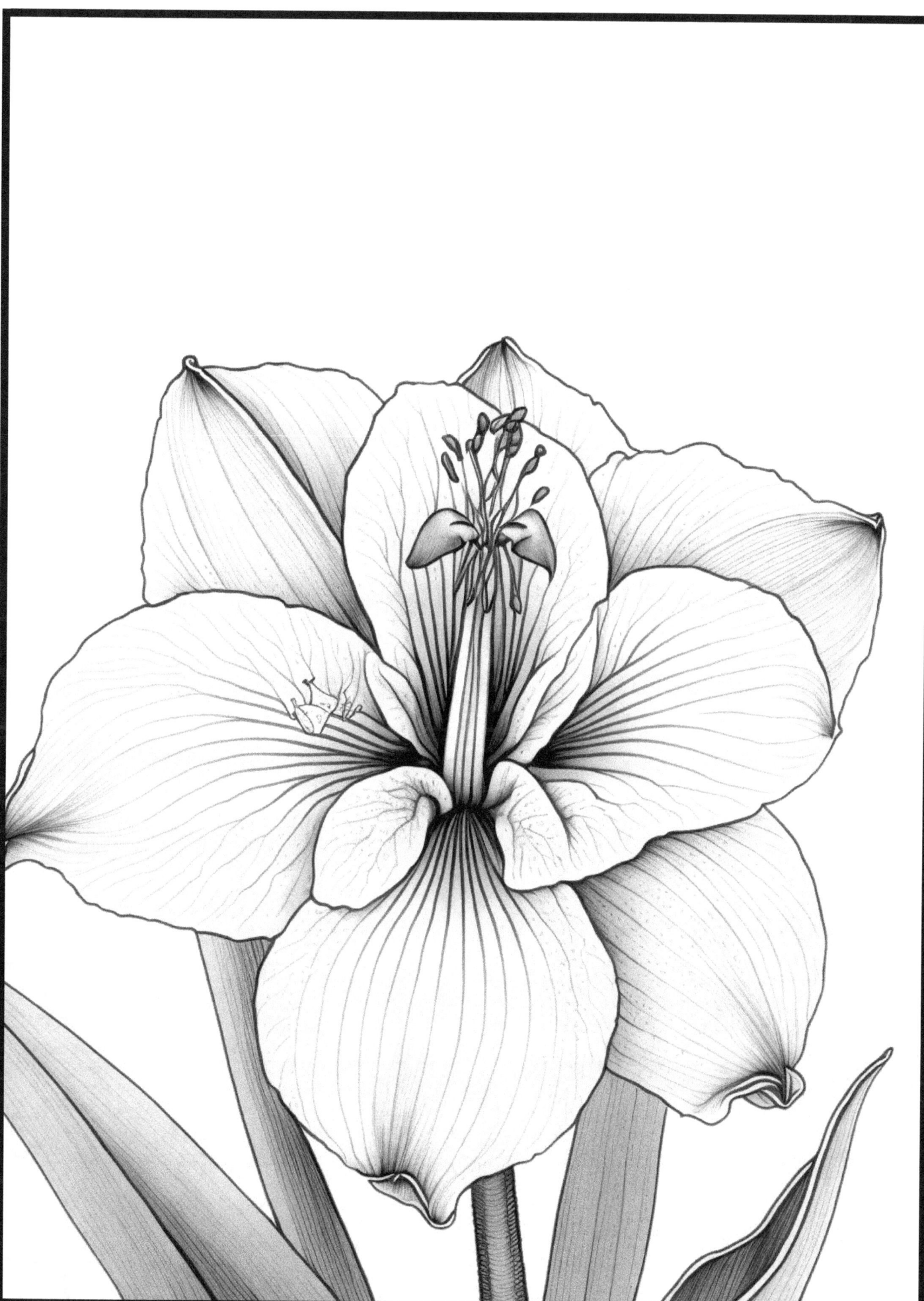

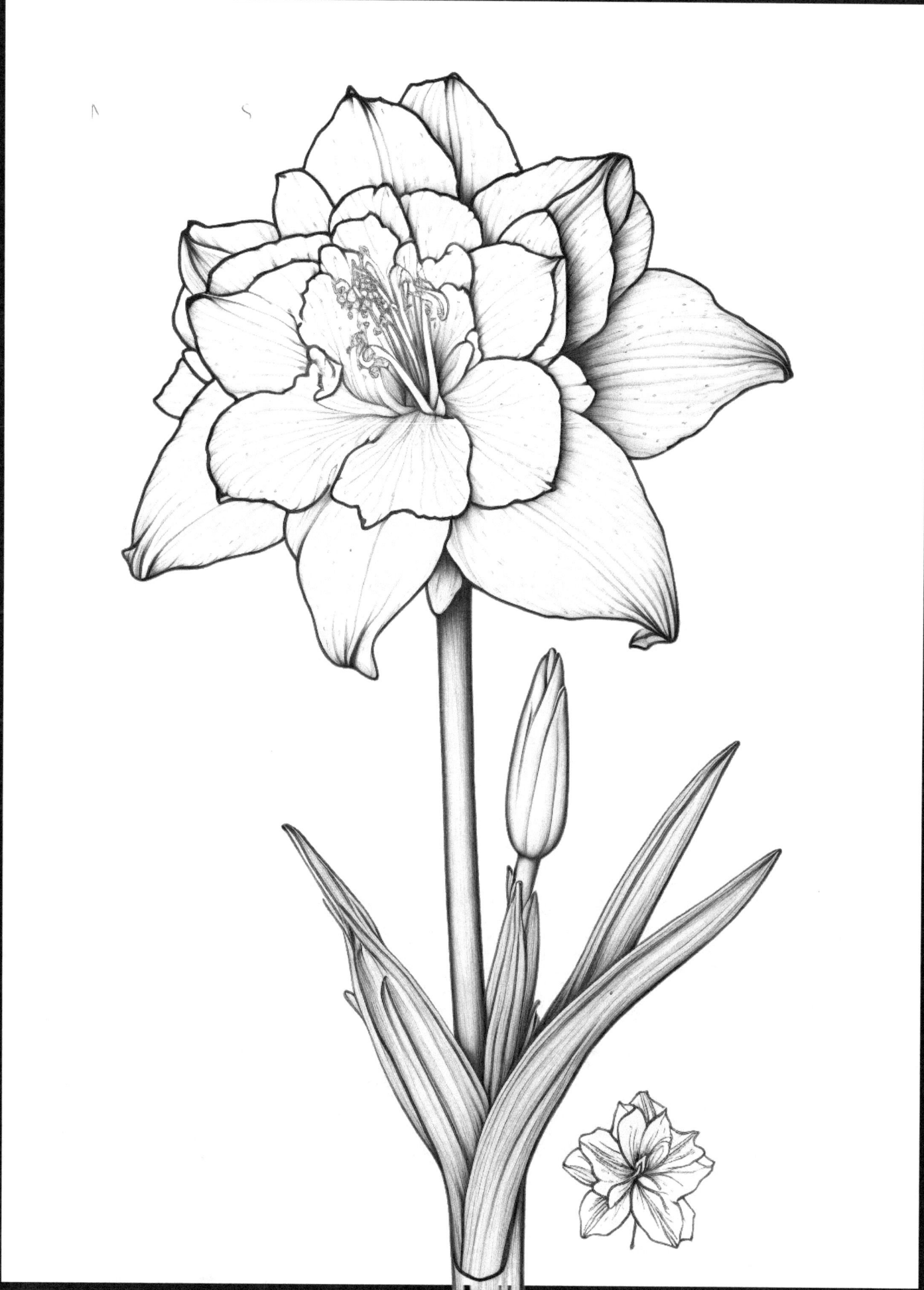

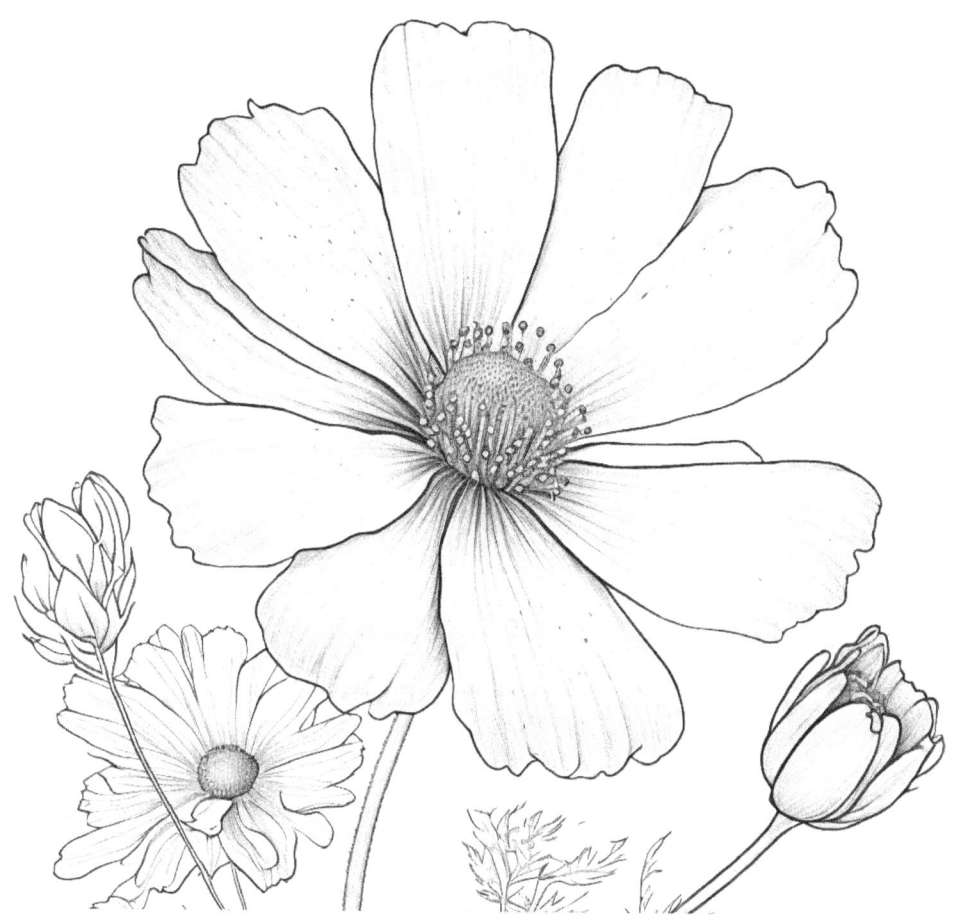

Thank you so much for your support in purchasing and coloring the "Flower Power: Coloring the Top 50 Blooms". Your encouragement and enthusiasm for this project means the world to me. I am thrilled to see that the book has helped you find moments of peace and relaxation. Your support has inspired me to continue creating art that brings joy and stress relief to people's lives.

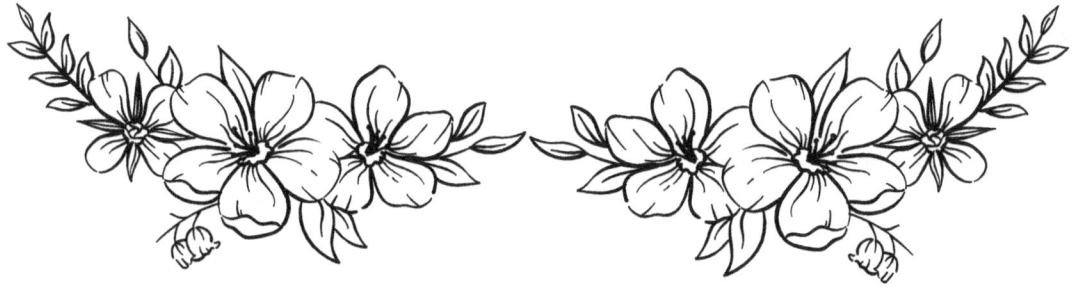